CHAUCER

A BEGINNER'S GUIDE

CATHERINE RICHARDSON

Hodder & Stoughton

A MEMBER OF THE HODDER HEADLINE GROUP

Orders: please contact Bookpoint Ltd, 130 Milton Park, Abingdon, Oxon OX14 4SB. Telephone: (44) 01235 400400, Fax: (44) 01235 400500. Lines are open from 9.00–6.00, Monday to Saturday, with a 24-hour message answering service. Email address: orders@bookpoint.co.uk

British Library Cataloguing in Publication Data
A catalogue record for this title is available from The British Library

ISBN 0 340 80361 4

First published 2001
Impression number   10 9 8 7 6 5 4 3 2 1
Year 2007 2006 2005 2004 2003 2002 2001

Illustrations by Steve Coots.
Cover photo from Corbis Images.
Typeset by Transet Limited, Coventry, England.
Printed in Great Britain for Hodder & Stoughton Educational, a division of Hodder Headline Plc, 338 Euston Road, London NW1 3BH by Cox & Wyman, Reading, Berks.

CONTENTS

How to use this book

The *Beginner's Guide* series aims to introduce readers to major writers of the past 500 years. It is assumed that readers will begin with little or no knowledge and will want to go on to explore the subject in other ways.

BEGIN READING THE AUTHOR

This book is a companion guide to Chaucer's major works, it is not a substitute for reading the books themselves. It would be useful if you read some of the works in parallel, so that you can put theory into practice. This book is divided into sections. After considering how to approach Chaucer's work and a brief biography, we go on to explore some of his main writings and themes before examining some critical approaches to the author. The survey finishes with suggestions for further reading and possible areas of further study.

HOW TO APPROACH UNFAMILIAR OR DIFFICULT TEXTS

Coming across a new writer may seem daunting, but do not be put off. The trick is to persevere. Much good writing is multi-layered and complex. It is precisely this diversity and complexity which makes literature rewarding and exhilarating.

Literature often needs to be read more than once, and in different ways. These ways can include: a leisurely and superficial reading to get the main ideas and narrative; a slower more detailed reading focusing on the nuances of the text, concentrating on what appear to be key passages; and reading in a random way, moving back and forth through the text to examine such things as themes, narrative or characterization.

In complex texts it may be necessary to read in short chunks. When it comes to tackling difficult words or concepts it is often enough to guess in context on the first reading, making a more detailed study using a dictionary or book of critical concepts on later reading. If you prefer to look up unusual words as you go along, be careful that you do not disrupt the flow of the text and your concentration.

VOCABULARY

You will see that Keywords and unfamiliar words are set in **bold** text. These words are defined and explained in the Glossary to be found at the back of the book. In order to help you further we have also included a summary at the end of each chapter.

You can read this introductory guide in its entirety or dip in wherever suits you. You can read it in any order. This book is a tool to help you appreciate a key figure in literature. We hope you enjoy reading it and find it useful.

✳ ✳ ✳ *SUMMARY* ✳ ✳ ✳

To maximize the use of this book:

- Read the author's work.

- Read it several times in different ways.

- Be open to innovative or unusual forms of writing.

- Persevere.

Rob Abbott & Charlie Bell

Why read Chaucer today?

Geoffrey Chaucer was born in the early 1340s in London, the son of a prosperous wine merchant. During the 60 years until his death in 1400, he was employed as a page, he worked in the royal household, and was sent abroad on many diplomatic missions. There are nearly 500 documents which record these and other details about his public life – all important for us as modern readers. We know more about Chaucer's career than we do about Shakespeare's, for instance, and we know much more about his life than we do about that of his contemporaries. The fact that Chaucer was sent abroad on missions indicates that he must have spoken several languages. All this information helps us to piece together why such a man would write such poems.

From the time he began writing people have been interested in Chaucer the artist as an individual, and many portraits of him survive. *The Canterbury Tales* are narrated by a pilgrim called Chaucer, inviting the reader to be interested in the poet himself, to ask questions about him. In Chaucer's case it is possible to satisfy the curiosity which we feel about the poet: it is possible to read his poems in the context of our knowledge about his life.

COMPARING DIFFERENT CULTURES

The fourteenth century, in which Chaucer was writing, has interesting parallels with and differences from our own. It was a period of rapid change in everyday life and of uncertainty and confusion about people's position within society. The Black Death decimated the country, killing 50 per cent of the population of London alone. The pre-existing structures of social, political and religious life struggled to cope with such radical changes: there were fewer governors and fewer people to govern. Ways of exercising and relating to authority changed, as war and social unrest took their toll. This was a very exciting but unsettling time to be alive. Reading Chaucer today allows us to examine how such crises affected the way a poet saw and wrote about his world.

There are clear points of contact for us with the fourteenth and fifteenth centuries: riots over the unpopular **poll tax**; sustained debates about the power and influence of the Church and the monarchy; and the threat of virulent and fatal diseases, which were only partly understood. These points of contact make the

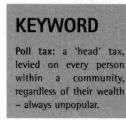

KEYWORD

Poll tax: a 'head' tax, levied on every person within a community, regardless of their wealth – always unpopular.

literature of the period particularly relevant and interesting. Reading Chaucer also makes it possible to explore the 'otherness' of the past, to be aware that people in the fourteenth and fifteenth centuries were very different from us. The poems he wrote reveal attitudes towards life and death and towards men and women which seem strange to us. We can compare the very different ways of thinking about and dealing with the issues which faced Chaucer's society and which now face ours.

GENDER ISSUES

Some issues were of particular concern to Chaucer and his society, and they are addressed again and again, in *The Canterbury Tales* and beyond, in his lesser known works such as *Troilus and Criseyde* and *The Legend of Good Women*. From the tale of the Wife of Bath to the tragedy of Criseyde's affair with Troilus, the relationship between the sexes is a recurring theme of Chaucer's work. The Wife claims boldly that 'no womman of no clerk is preysed', that as it is only men who write stories they are bound to cast women as the villains. 'By God', she says, 'if wommen hadden writen stories/ As clerks han [had]…They wolde han writen of men moore wickkednesse' than all the men in the world put together could redress. Through his portrayal of a woman complaining about the misogyny of male writers, Chaucer is able to comment on his own activity as a man writing stories about women.

HOW MEDIEVAL SOCIETY WORKS

The Wife of Bath is one of Chaucer's most famous characters because he makes her appear more than a stereotypical garrulous old woman: he adds lots of little details which give us a clear image of her face, clothes and manner. Reading Chaucer means being introduced to other such characters who vividly represent nearly the whole of medieval society between them, and seeing how they relate to one another. There are morally suspect monks and prioresses; disgusting cooks and argumentative millers; honest parsons and ploughmen; courtly ladies and their knightly lovers.

AN INFLUENCE ON ALL LATER POETRY

We also need to read Chaucer if we want to understand why poetry takes the forms it does today. T. S. Eliot opens his poem 'The Waste Land' with the words 'April is the cruellest month, breeding/ Lilacs out of the dead land, mixing/ Memory and desire, stirring/ Dull roots with spring rain.' In doing so, he makes reference to the beginning of *The Canterbury Tales*: 'Whan that Aprill with his shoures soote/ The droughte of March had perced to the roote'. Eliot's poem starts with Chaucer because Chaucer's work is in many ways the beginning of poetry in English as we know it. In the period in which Chaucer was writing, English was primarily a spoken language. When things were written down – histories, legal documents, treatises or poems – they were generally recorded either in French or in Latin. Although English had been a literary language for a century, Chaucer was regarded, even by his contemporaries, as its most distinguished exponent. Reading Chaucer means reading poetry in a written language which was novel, interesting in its own right, and full of the most exciting possibilities for the artist.

Although Chaucer's medium was English, the stories about which he wrote came from classical and European traditions. They are varied in their provenance and their **genre**. In *The Canterbury Tales* alone there are bawdy

KEYWORD

Genre: a kind, form, or type of literature with its own unique set of stylistic features.

stories which present absurd sexual antics, there are tales of magic and of faery, there are moral and cautionary tales, and there are allegorical stories of patience and fortitude. Such diversity of mood, of style and of the response demanded from a reader gives Chaucer the flexibility to approach fundamental questions in a wide variety of ways.

* * * SUMMARY * * *

Chaucer is relevant to us today because:

• he influenced the development of English as a literary language

• he is the first poet whose life we can explore in detail

• he responds to the changing value systems of his time

• he explores issues of gender and the relationship between the sexes.

• he employs a huge variety of styles and genres.

How to approach Chaucer's work

A UNIQUE READING EXPERIENCE

If you've never read Chaucer before, think of this as a completely unique and exciting experience. If you have read him before, and have found it hard, then this chapter suggests ways of making it easier. The first thing you have to do is to forget all your expectations and preconceptions about Chaucer himself, and also about reading in general. You are entering a different world of reading, a world with no books as we think of them; a world before printing had been invented; before the huge majority of people could read; even before most of those who *could* read expected *what* they read to be written in English. You are entering the fourteenth century...

'And smale foweles maken melodie, that slepen al the night with open ye'

THE CANTERBURY TALES

Chaucer's most famous work is *The Canterbury Tales*. It is a collection of stories told by pilgrims on their way to the shrine of St Thomas Becket in Canterbury cathedral. The General Prologue to *The*

Canterbury Tales introduces each of the pilgrims in turn. It opens with a description of spring, the time when Chaucer tells us that people's thoughts turn to going on pilgrimage. Here is a part of that description. Read it through and see how many words you can identify:

> Whan that Aprill with his shoures soote
> The droghte of March hath perced to the roote,
> And bathed every veine in swich licour
> Of which vertu engendred is the flour...
> And smale foweles maken melodie,
> That slepen al the night with open ye
> (So priketh hem nature in hir corages);
> Thanne longen folk to goon on pilgrimages

Don't panic!

The first thing to do when reading this passage is not to panic! Reading Chaucer isn't like reading a modern novel, it is a much much slower process. Don't expect to be able to understand the lines the first, second, or even third time. This is part of the pleasure of reading Chaucer, slowly enjoying the language he uses.

Look at this translation:

> *When April with his sweet showers*
> *Has pierced the drought of March to the root*
> *And bathed every veine [of the plants] in such liquid*
> *By which power the flower is created...*
> *And small birds make melodie,*
> *That sleep all night with open eye*
> *So nature goads them in their desires*
> *Then people long to go on pilgrimages.*

It is not nearly as appealing, it doesn't give the same impression of the vitality and energy of spring. Phrases like 'shoures soote' and 'maken melodie' have a very particular rhythm, and that rhythm is a large part of the way Chaucer communicates a spring-like feeling to the reader.

This is why you should always read Chaucer's poetry as he wrote it (using a translation as well at first to get you started if you like) – understanding the verse is as much about hearing it as it as about knowing what the words mean. Sometimes an impression of meaning is more important than being able to translate every word exactly.

Forget about spelling...

Probably the first thing that you will have noticed about the passage is that when Chaucer was writing there was no concept of spelling as we understand it today: the same word could be spelt in many different ways, and most of these variations are different again from the spelling we're used to. This is because words are spelt as they sound, as you say them. So the second thing to do when reading this passage is to try reading it out loud.

When you do this you'll realize that Chaucer's English not only looks different, it sounds very different from our own. Scholars have tried to decipher how the poems would have sounded when Chaucer read them, and these differences in pronunciation partly explain why the words are written down so differently from our own version of English. It doesn't *matter* how you pronounce the words, but if you are interested in reading about, and even hearing, how they originally sounded, then look at Chapter 8.

Look out for detail...

Chaucer's style in this passage is known as 'High Style'. One of the skills which is particularly admired in High Style is the expansion of descriptions to make them as long and as evocative as possible. Chaucer begins his description of spring with 'When': '*Whan* that Aprill with his shoures soote', but he only tells the reader what happens when April pierces the drought of March 11 lines later – people long to on pilgrimages. Now try reading the whole description from start to finish:

Whan that Aprill with his shoures soote [*sweet showers*]
The droghte of March hath perced to the roote,
And bathed every veine in swich licour [*such liquid*]
Of which vertu [*by which power*] engendred is the flour;
Whan Zephirus eek with his sweete breeth
Inspired hath in every holt and heeth
The tendre croppes, and the yonge sonne
Hath in the Ram his half cours yronne,

[*When Zephirus (the west wind) with his sweet breath*
Has breathed life in every grove and field
To the tender shoots, and the young sun
Has run half of his course in the Ram (the sign of Aries, entered after the
vernal equinox)]

And smale foweles [*birds*] maken melodie,
That slepen al the night with open [*e*]ye
(So priketh hem nature [*nature goads them*] in hir corages [*desires*]);
Thanne longen folk to goon [*go*] on pilgrimages

This kind of style is very different from the pared down prose we are used to, in newspapers for instance. Again, it is important to be prepared to read slowly, to enjoy the complexities of the descriptions offered in the poetry. It is also important to take pleasure in Chaucer's cleverness – his inventive use of language and detail.

Look out for Chaucer's word pictures...

Reading Chaucer also means thinking about language as a very *visual* way of communicating. Close your eyes and imagine spring now, as Chaucer described it. He is using language to build up a picture in the reader's mind's eye, and that is why his descriptions are so powerful. As you go on to read about all the characters who are making their way to Canterbury on pilgrimage, you can think about them riding through Kent in the spring.

As he introduces each of the pilgrims who are going to Canterbury, Chaucer tells us what they do and what they look like. So the poem is divided up into smaller sections which are like verbal paintings. This makes the General Prologue a great place to start reading Chaucer. Spend as long as you like on each pilgrim.

✳ ✳ ✳ SUMMARY ✳ ✳ ✳

To get the most out of Chaucer's work:

● Read slowly, be prepared to read each section several times.

● Read out loud, enjoy the sounds of the words as well as their meaning.

● Think about what the words make you see – Chaucer's detailed word pictures of pilgrims.

---

3 Biography and social background

WHY DO WE NEED TO KNOW WHO CHAUCER WAS?

Why is it important to know who Chaucer was? Does it make any difference to the way we read his poems to know where he was born, or who his father was? If this was a book about Chaucer's contemporary, the poet who wrote *Gawain and the Green Knight*, there wouldn't *be* a chapter on his life because we don't even know what his name was.

Some literary critics warn us about the dangers of being too interested in the author of a text. They say that this suggests that a poem like *The Canterbury Tales* has only one authoritative meaning, the one that Chaucer intended, rather than a variety of meanings which different readers create when they read the poem. Such critics are also concerned that being interested in the author leads us to think of the poem as a unique product of his 'genius', rather than a piece of writing which is influenced by other pieces of writing, and made possible *because* of the author's knowledge of those other works.

These arguments are important and we should bear them in mind when we think about the kind of poetry Chaucer wrote, and the way in which those who read it have interpreted it. The arguments about the importance of authors also suggest that, in order to understand what Chaucer's poems might have meant to their

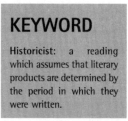

KEYWORD

Historicist: a reading which assumes that literary products are determined by the period in which they were written.

original readers, we need to situate them within their historical context – to discover what was happening when he was writing. Getting to grips with *The Canterbury Tales* involves seeing them as a product of both Chaucer's imagination *and* the concerns and preoccupations of the fourteenth century. This is known as a **historicist** approach, and you can read more about it in Chapter 7.

WHAT WAS A 'MEDIEVAL AUTHOR'?

It is important to understand that the whole concept of 'the author' of a work of literature was changing in the period in which Chaucer was writing. Before Chaucer's time authors were content to remain anonymous. This is hard for us to imagine: we see authors on the television and in the newspapers all the time, and we often know quite a lot about the person who wrote a text before we even read it. This idea would have seemed very strange in the fourteenth century because the writer wasn't considered important, and people rarely knew who he was (and it almost always was 'he'). Texts gained authority because they were seen to be *passing on* knowledge, rather than *creating* it, and the concept of an 'invisible' author – more like a translator – helped to maintain this impression. But things were changing.

Medieval thinkers developed theories about the relationship between authors and their work. Prior to Chaucer's period, 'authorship' tended to be thought of as a role – like a character in a play – a role of authority represented by the character who was 'speaking' the text. Nobody thought of a real person sitting down with a quill to write. When *The Canterbury Tales* was written, those thinkers were beginning to show an interest in the author as an individual, as a real person outside of the text rather than just a voice from within it.

WAS CHAUCER A TYPICAL MEDIEVAL AUTHOR?

Chaucer was clearly involved in these changes: it is easy to see this because he keeps telling his readers all about himself! The narrator of *The Canterbury Tales* is a pilgrim who is called Chaucer. After the Prioress has told her tale, the host who accompanies the pilgrims on their journey turns to Chaucer the pilgrim and asks him to tell a tale:

> Sey now somwhat, syn oother folk han sayd;
> Telle us a tale of myrthe, and that anon.
>
> *Say something now, since other people have;*
> *Tell us a tale of mirth straightaway.*

This invites us to wonder how much Chaucer the pilgrim is like the author of the poem. When he expresses an opinion, are we listening to what the real Chaucer was thinking? But Chaucer also sends himself up and mocks our attempts to see this character as representing the author himself. Half-way into his tale the host interrupts him:

Namoore of this, for Goddes dignitee…
Thy drasty rymyng is nat worth a toord!

No more of this for God's dignity…
Your crappy rhyming isn't worth a turd!

Chaucer the pilgrim is so bad at poetry that nobody wants to hear his tale.

What did Chaucer look like?

The host also describes Chaucer the pilgrim physically. The portrait he gives again leaves us wondering how similar this character is to the author himself:

He in the waast is shape as wel as I;
This were a popet in an arm t'embrace
For any womman, smal and fair of face.
He semeth elvyssh by his contenaunce,
For unto no wight dooth he daliaunce.

He's shaped as well as I am in the waist;
He's a little doll to cuddle
For any woman, slender and fair of face.
He seems elvish [mysterious] by his countenance
Because he's sociable to no one.

By leaving the reader wondering whether Chaucer himself was indeed mysterious, shy and like a child's 'poppet' or doll, the author once again makes us imagine the person writing, the author who is controlling what we read.

The invisible medieval author

BIOGRAPHICAL DETAILS

The 'real' Geoffrey Chaucer was born some time in the 1340s, the son of John Chaucer, a London wine merchant. Although his family were members of the merchant classes, rather than the gentry, they were fairly wealthy because there was a good deal of money in wine. Most of the information we have about Chaucer's life doesn't refer to his poetry, but to the other jobs he held. They suggest some of the areas of life of which he had experience.

He was what we might loosely call a civil servant, as well as a courtier, a page to members of the royal household. From 1374 to 1386, the year before he began *The Canterbury Tales*, he was a customs controller for wool in the Port of London, checking that everyone paid their taxes on their imports and exports, and trying to prevent smuggling. He was also a Clerk of the King's Works, which meant he looked after all the royal buildings, making sure they were kept in good order.

Chaucer was probably born in Thames Street, the centre of the wine trade near the Thames in the heart of London which was, even then, by far the largest city in England. But London was still small in comparison to continental cities. Whilst on diplomatic business, Chaucer would have seen some of these centres of learning and literary production as he travelled to Italy, France and Spain. Some of the continental influences on his writing are explored in the following chapters.

LIFE IN THE FOURTEENTH CENTURY

What connections can be made between *The Canterbury Tales* and the society in which Chaucer lived and worked? We can use the portraits of the pilgrims as illustrations of the broad differences in social status within fourteenth-century life.

The differences between the pilgrims show the complicated distinctions between middling and high social status in this period. But comparing them to other individuals described in *The Canterbury Tales* shows clearly that the most important divisions in Chaucer's society were between those of high and those of low social status. We're all familiar with this basic division from stories such as Robin Hood, but what did it actually mean, on a day-to-day basis? Since a small percentage of the population held most of the wealth, their daily life was completely different from the existence of those beneath them.

What did people eat?

Part of Chaucer's portrayal of the Franklin, a type of provincial gentleman, describes the kind of hospitality which he offered:

> Withoute bake mete was nevere his hous
> Of fissh and flessh, and that so plentevous,
> It snewed in his hous of mete and drinke;
> Of alle deyntees that men koude thinke.
> After the sondry sesons of the yeer,
> So chaunged he his mete and his soper.

> *His house was never without the pies*
> *Of fish and meat, which were so plenteous*
> *That it snowed meat and drink in his house*
> *Of all delicacies that men could imagine.*
> *In response to the different seasons of the year*
> *He changed his food and his menus.*

In contrast to this blizzard of plenty in the Franklin's house, the poor widow, in the tale told by the Nun's Priest, lives in a much more modest residence:

> Ful sooty was hire bour and eek hir halle,
> In which she eet ful many a sklendre meel.
> Of poynaunt sauce hir neded never a deel.
> No deyntee morsel passed thurgh hir throte;
> Hir diete was accordant to hir cote.

> *Very sooty was her bedroom and also her hall,*
> *In which she ate many a slender meal.*
> *She never needed any spicy sauce.*
> *No dainty morsel passed through her throat;*
> *Her diet was in accordance with her small farm.*

In the period in which Chaucer was writing, the feasts of the nobility were becoming even more elaborate, with many different courses and dishes. A shopping list for a royal feast which survives from 1387, and which Chaucer might well have attended because of his position at court, mentions 14 oxen in salt, 120 sheep's heads, 50 swans, 10 dozen curlew and, amongst many other items, 11 thousand eggs! Chaucer's other jobs gave him access to this world of excess, to occasions which individuals like the poor widow he describes could hardly have been able to imagine.

'It snewed in his hous of mete and drinke'

How did people behave?

More money didn't only mean more food, it also meant different ways
of behaving. The poor widow wouldn't have concerned herself with
table manners, but Chaucer's description of the Prioress shows how
important behaviour was in distinguishing between the rich and the
poor:

> She leet no morsel from hir lippes falle,
> Ne wette hir fyngres in hir sauce depe;
> Wel koude she carie a morsel and wel kepe
> That no drope ne fille upon hire brest.
> In curteisie was set ful muchel hir lest.

> *She let no morsel from her lips fall,*
> *Nor wet her fingers in her sauce deep;*
> *She knew how to carry a morsel and take care*
> *That no drop fell on her breast*
> *Her greatest pleasure was in good manners.*

So the rich didn't only eat better, they acted differently too – they
thought of themselves as more refined and took pride in the kinds of
behaviour which accompanied a different lifestyle. You could also tell
them apart from the poor immediately, just by looking at them.
Chaucer frequently describes his pilgrims in terms of their clothing, for
instance the young Squire:

> Embrouded was he, as it were a meede
> Al ful of fresshe floures, whyte and reede.

> *He was embroidered as though he was a meadow*
> *All full of fresh flowers, white and red.*

Or the Wife of Bath:

> Hir coverchiefs ful fyne weren of ground;
> I dorste swere they weyeden ten pound
> That on a Sonday weren upon hir heed.

Hir hosen weren of fyn scarlet reed,
Ful streite yteyd, and shoes ful moyste and newe.

Her headcoverings were of very fine texture;
I dare swear they weighed ten pounds
Which she wore on her head on a Sunday.
Her stockings were of fine scarlet
Closely laced, and her shoes very supple and new.

The plain working clothes of the poor, often made of material which they had woven themselves, were very different indeed.

THEN EVERYTHING CHANGED...

The plague

For the first part of the fourteenth century, society was very inflexible – the rich were rich, the poor were poor, and the distinctions between them were very clear indeed – two separate worlds. Then the Black Death came. In 1347 a ship arrived in the Sicilian port of Messina filled with corpses and dying men. This plague, which had already affected India and the Middle and Near East, crept gradually along the trade routes towards Northern Europe. In June 1348 it arrived on the shores of Britain, probably at Melcombe in Dorset. Within the next few months, up to two million people died in England out of a population of four to five million. The infection began as a swelling in the armpits or the groin and death followed within two to three days.

The tightly packed streets where the poor lived ensured that the disease spread quickly from house to house. Those in the direst economic circumstances were particularly badly affected because they lived closest to their neighbours and were unable to escape to more isolated areas. Death, however, was no respecter of wealth or rank. Manuscripts depicting the three living and the three dead became popular. These contained images of three wealthy and important people meeting three decomposing corpses. When asked who they are, the corpses reveal themselves to be the wealthy people as they will be in the future,

stripped of the earthly trappings of clothing and even flesh, so that in
death they look identical to the poor.

*'Such as I was you are, and such as I am you will be. Wealth, honour and power are of no
value at the hour of your death'*

Chaucer's grandparents and many of his other relatives died as the
plague hit London. His father, John, unexpectedly inherited a
considerable amount of property as half of his family was wiped out.
This kind of unexpected benefit shook the carefully constructed social
divisions between people, and it made social mobility inevitable.

The poll tax riot

Economic change was also bound to follow. Considerably fewer
workers began to demand much higher wages to work the land.
Government tried to control these increases and they tried to raise
more money for wars in France from a much smaller population. The
tax they came up with was the first tax not to discriminate between the
rich and the poor – it was called the poll, or head, tax.

The 14-year-old King Richard II found himself dealing with a riot
which has since become known as the Peasants' Revolt. In fact, it was
probably started by those who had made comparative fortunes by the
rapid redistribution of wealth which accompanied the death of their
relatives in the plague. Not the peasants, in other words, but those who
had managed to rise above that low social position, and were afraid of
returning to it.

The rebels targeted their aggression carefully – destroying documents and accounts to bring confusion to administration, and finally murdering the Archbishop of Canterbury. However, when their leader was killed, the young Richard offered himself to the rebels as their captain, and he proceeded to reassert his authority strongly.

What does *The Canterbury Tales* have to do with these changes?

So how different was society in the 1380s? Chaucer began to write *The Canterbury Tales* after a period of substantial social unrest and when the changes caused by the Black Death were still a clear memory, not least for people like himself who still held the property of relatives who had died as a result of the disease. *The Canterbury Tales* is a poem which examines, in its opening Prologue, the way in which society functions. The descriptions of

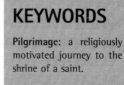

KEYWORDS

Pilgrimage: a religiously motivated journey to the shrine of a saint.

Lollardy: fourteenth-century heretical beliefs in a variety of corruptions in the organization and worship of the medieval Catholic Church.

the pilgrims are organized by profession. Between them, they represent a whole society, with men and women, religious and secular occupations, and the nobility and those below them all joining together on a **pilgrimage**.

The poem itself, then, poses questions about society, it tries to establish how communities work now that everything has changed and it uses the occasion of a pilgrimage because it is a situation in which all those different kinds of people might come together. However, there's one other problem in this period and it influences our understanding of Chaucer's choice of subject matter.

Why did Chaucer choose a pilgrimage?

Some people were beginning to criticize the Church. They didn't doubt the existence of God, but they did query the way in which the Church told people to worship him. These people came to be known as **Lollards**. They had lots of problems with the religion of the time,

Catholicism, from the fact that the Bible was always written and read in Latin, a language which only the social elite understood, to the elaborate imagery of parish churches. They also thought pilgrimage was against the teachings of the Bible. They thought it was a waste of money and believed that it was often used as an excuse for indulging in all sorts of exciting sins on the way – far away from friends and neighbours who might tell tales.

The pilgrims tell their tales on the journey to the shrine of St Thomas Becket in Canterbury cathedral, one of the foremost shrines in medieval England. When Chaucer chose his subject for *The Canterbury Tales* there were two views of pilgrimage. The traditional view was that it was an important part of religious practice, a spiritual journey which offered a metaphor for the Christian soul's journey through life to heaven. This was contrasted with the Lollard view that it led to sin and debauchery. When you read the poem, you need to think about these competing ideas and about the contribution which Chaucer is making to them. Does he criticize the Church, and if so how?

Reading *The Canterbury Tales* now that you know something about the period in which it was written should completely change the poem's meaning. If we didn't know about the changes which had taken place in the fourteenth century, we might think that Chaucer's work had no political or social role to play. Understanding the way the poem engages with contemporary issues makes us read the work much more carefully and underlines its importance.

HOW DID CHAUCER DEVELOP THE ENGLISH LANGUAGE?

It all started with 1066...

In 1065, chronicles report that there were great gales in England. Then Edward the Confessor, the saintly old king of England, died. There were comets blazing in the sky and his successor Harold had bad dreams. These ominous signs are the chroniclers' way of describing the momentousness of what happened next.

In October 1066, Harold had just managed to fight off an invasion by the Norwegians. However, the day after his success, with his armies still in the north of England, the Normans set sail for England with 400 warships, landing on the south coast. We all know how the story ended from the Bayeux Tapestry, which shows Harold falling in battle with an arrow sticking out of his eye.

William of Normandy was crowned as King of England on Christmas Day 1066. He now ruled a kingdom which reached from the top of England down to the Pyrenees – a truly multicultural nation. Half of the English nobility were dead after the two battles of 1066, and William had rewarded his faithful French nobles with grants of land in his new territories. Overnight, a huge change came over the men who controlled England, one which would influence its native literature for centuries: they now spoke French.

French-speaking Englishmen

Although Chaucer was writing three centuries later, this fundamental change affected him greatly. Ranulph Higden wrote about schooling in the 1360s:

> Children in school, contrary to the usage and custom of other nations, are compelled to leave their own language and to construe their lessons and tasks in French… gentlemen's children are taught to speak French from the time that they are rocked in their cradles, and can talk and play with a child's toy.

> Trevisa's translation of Ranulph Higden, *Polychronicon*, translated from Derek Pearsall, *Chaucer to Spenser* (Blackwell, 1999), p. 230.

So Chaucer was probably taught French as a child and, as this quote shows, speaking English marked you out socially – it suggested that you were of a lower social status than those who spoke French. For instance we are given an important detail to explain the status of the Prioress in *The Canterbury Tales*: 'Frenssh she spak ful faire and fetisly'.

English was becoming more important

However, in Chaucer's lifetime things were changing. By the 1380s French was no longer being taught in schools, and English was even becoming the language of government. The Chancellor had opened the Parliament of 1366 with a speech in English – the first time since 1066. Legal language was changing, too – in 1362 it was made law that all cases should be 'pleaded, shewed, defended, answered, debated, and judged in the English tongue' (*Statute of Pleading*). These were very important changes for the status of English – they made it an appropriate language in which to conduct significant national business.

A suitable language for poetry

English was also becoming a suitable language for literature. Men like John Gower, were writing in Latin and French as well as English, making it just one of several options. Gower's *Confessio Amantis* was a very important English work because it was commissioned by King Richard himself. So the important difference in Chaucer's time is not that people suddenly started writing in English, or even that they suddenly started writing *poetry* in English, but that they started to do so for an *aristocratic audience*. This gave the language a very different kind of status. It became appropriate as a literary language for the poetry of kings, which is very different from the language which is spoken in alehouses!

The language of poetry is different from spoken English

As an elite literary language, English had to change. Compare the language of any poem to spoken English and you will see the problem which authors faced in the fourteenth century. Chaucer's High Style, mentioned ealier, was one way of making everyday spoken English into poetry – through extended description.

Chaucer's skill in *The Canterbury Tales* lies partly in combining these elevated forms of speech with dialogue in colloquial spoken English. The prologue to the Miller's Tale demonstrates this point. The previous tale is received with proper decorum:

Whan that the Knyght had thus his tale ytoold,
In al the compaignie nas ther yong ne oold
That he ne seyde it was a noble storie

When the Knight had told his tale,
There was no one in the party, young or old
Who didn't say it was a noble story

This gracious reception is soon interrupted, however, by the Miller. He is drunk, and insists on telling the next tale although it is not his turn. He swears:

…'By armes, and by blood and bones,
I kan a noble tale for the nones
With which I wol now quite the Knyghtes tale.'

… 'By [Christ's] arms, and by blood and bones
I know a noble tale
With which I will now match the Knight's tale'.

By combining the elevated language of the Knight's Tale with the language of the Miller (who has literally come from the pub!), Chaucer gives a sophisticated texture and liveliness to his poem.

Chaucer spoke London English

There is one other important thing to note about Chaucer's particular use of English: he was a Southerner. Born in London, he spoke a language which was influenced by the Court and by London's status as a centre of learning. However, then as now, there were many other dialects spoken in the country. At the time, these were divided into Southern, Midlands and Northern English, and they were thought to date from the time when the different areas were settled by different peoples – the Angles, the Jutes and the Saxons.

John of Trevisa describes the language of the inhabitants of York as:

…so sharp, piercing and grating and unshapely that we Southern men can hardly understand that language. I suppose that this is because they are nigh to foreign men [the Scots]…who speak strangely, and also because the kings of England dwell always far from that country.

Trevisa's translation of Higden's *Polychronicon*, translated from Pearsall
ed., p. 231.

Compare the description of spring from *The Canterbury Tales* with which this book started with the following description of a winter landscape from *Gawain and the Green Knight*:

Bi a mounte on the morne meryly he rydes
Into a forest ful dep, that derly was wylde,
Highe hilles on uche a halve, and holtwodes under
Of hore okes ful hoge a hundreth togeder.
The hasel and the hawthorne were harled al samen,
With roghe raged mosse rayled aywhere,
With mony bryddes unblythe upon bare twyges,
That pitosly ther piped for pyne of the colde.

By a hill in the morning merrily he rides
Into a deep forest, that was wonderfully wild,
High hills on each side, and woods below
Of huge grey oaks, a hundred together.
The hazel and the hawthorn were tangled together,
With rough shaggy moss growing everywhere,
With may unhappy birds on bare twigs,
That piteously sang there for pain of [caused by] the cold.

This passage is difficult partly because the author of the poem probably came from the north-west Midlands, so his vocabulary is different from Chaucer's. The version of English which we are used to has developed from London English so, although Chaucer might seem hard to understand, he's often much easier than his contemporary poets.

The poem is also very hard to read because the traditional poetry of the north was **alliterative verse**. This type of verse rhymes within the lines: it is defined at the start of *Gawain* as having 'letteres loken', or linked. The repetition of letters within the lines (That **p**itosly ther **p**iped for **p**yne of the colde) gives a very different effect from Chaucer's poetry, which is often end-rhymed.

KEYWORDS

Gawain and the Green Knight: a fourteenth century alliterative poem about a large green knight who challenges Gawain to a beheading game on New Year's Day.

Alliterative verse: poetry in which consonants or stressed syllables are repeated.

London English becomes standard

By the fifteenth century the English spoken in London had become the standard dialect for all written English, which is why Chaucer's work is so much more familiar to us than that of his northern contemporaries. It became associated with the Court, and therefore with power: it literally became the King's English.

So to a certain extent, Chaucer was in the right place at the right time. He was living and writing around the seat of government at the end of at least a hundred years of the gradually increasing status of written English. But the appeal of the poems he wrote, his skill in using and developing the potential of English as a literary language, also contributed considerably to the increased status of the language. The history of Chaucer's poetry and the development of our language are inextricably tied up with one another.

✴ ✴ ✴ *SUMMARY* ✴ ✴ ✴

- The authors of medieval texts had traditionally been anonymous, but Chaucer was different.

- Medieval society had been characterized by sharp distinctions between the rich and the poor.

- Plague, religious change and social and political unrest were changing the fabric of society.

- The subject which Chaucer chose for *The Canterbury Tales* was a contentious one at the time.

- Although people spoke English on a day-to-day basis, French had been the language of England's rulers since 1066.

- By the time Chaucer was writing in the 1380s, English was becoming an administrative language, but also a suitable medium for elite poetry.

- 'London English' became the standard dialect a century after Chaucer's death.

- Chaucer was in the right place at the right time, and he and literary English made each other more popular.

Major works 4

This chapter concentrates on The General Prologue and several of the individual stories within *The Canterbury Tales*, but it also contains information about two of Chaucer's other poems, *Troilus and Criseyde* and *The Legend of Good Women*. The next chapter, on Major Themes, will investigate the preoccupations and ideas which these works share.

RE-TELLING TALES

Most of the stories Chaucer writes about in the poems discussed in this chapter had already been told by the time he came to write about them. This is another important difference between medieval fiction and our own.

What is admirable and impressive about a medieval story-teller is 'the way he tells them' – how he alters the essential elements of a narrative in different and interesting ways. So, seeing how a familiar story will develop is a large part of the pleasure of reading for a medieval audience, and the author's skills in description and the presentation of characters are aspects which would have been of particular interest to them.

We are still familiar with the gist of some of these stories today. The Clerk's Tale, for instance, is a kind of Cinderella story, and the Wife of Bath's Tale is a quirky version of the Frog Prince – in this case a frog princess. But in the case of a poem like *Troilus and Criseyde* it is not just the outline of the story which is recognizable, but the characters and locations, too. Chaucer took the story from Boccaccio's *Filostrato*, written about 50 years previously in the 1330s. It was told again, over 200 years after Chaucer, by Shakespeare. Many of these tales come from continental authors, sometimes translated by them from classical sources. Chaucer's frequent trips abroad on diplomatic business must have given him the opportunity to increase his knowledge of the works of these authors.

THE GENERAL PROLOGUE TO *THE CANTERBURY TALES*

By the time Chaucer came to write *The Canterbury Tales*, near the end of his career, he had learned a lot about French courtly verse and about the work of Italian poets like Boccaccio. He was skilled in the styles of continental poetry, but he was becoming increasingly interested in a different kind of subject matter: the representation of everyday English life.

The Prologue is surprisingly 'English'

The Prologue to *The Canterbury Tales* was probably written between 1388 and 1392, at the same time as some of the earlier tales. It begins with the description of spring which you have already read, and you can see the continental influence in the elegant and elevated language, punctuated by classical allusions, for example, Zephyrus's sweet breath.

The medieval reader would probably have expected this evocation to lead to an encounter with the classical gods. However, Chaucer turns these expectations on their head by setting the scene in a pub in present-day Southwark, and fills it with an inn-keeper and some pilgrims rather than the gods.

Such unexpected surprises are an important part of the way Chaucer constructs his poem. Several other poems exist which are constructed as a series of tales told by different tellers, but the idea of using pilgrimage as a structure is also unique. So Chaucer's poem is a complex and excitingly different interweaving of classical models and English life; traditional stories and surprising innovations.

How 'real' are the pilgrims?

The descriptions of the pilgrims themselves are influenced by a long tradition of literary portraiture, where individuals are described physically and in terms of their daily activities. Chaucer's characters are also influenced by the familiar **types** of what is called **estates satire**.

KEYWORDS

Type: a person or character who serves as a representative of a group of people.

Estates satire: the use of stereotype to show the worst or best of different occupations or ranks.

Estates satire describes representatives of different occupations who epitomize either the best or, more often, the worst way of performing their particular job. These portraits weren't very subtle, as you can imagine, and they included figures such as the 'thieving miller' or the 'deceiving friar'.

We are still familiar with these kinds of stereotypes today, for instance, the corrupt politician, or the woman driver. They are an important part of the way in which we understand how our own society works: how we translate an infinite variety of individuals into groups with similar characteristics whose behaviour we like to think we can predict. Problems occur only when people come face to face with an individual and expect them to conform to such a type.

This is important because Chaucer's version of estates literature is, of course, different. Instead of presenting an obvious **allegory** of vice or virtue, where the pilgrims as a group demonstrate the very best or the very worst of character traits, he gives us individualized characters who appear to be too peculiar or extraordinary to represent a whole group. As readers we are often unsure whether we should respond to them as individuals or as stereotypes and whether Chaucer is making a point about their profession as a whole or not.

> **KEYWORD**
>
> Allegory: a narrative which can be understood on several different levels.

Chaucer expects us to understand these characters in relation to what we know about ideal parsons, or merchants, or prioresses. It is only when we see these individuals against the model that we can judge them morally, in relation to how well they are fulfilling their role in society.

How does Chaucer construct his pilgrim portraits?

As you read the portraits, look out for the techniques Chaucer uses to form your opinion of the characters. He is very careful about the order in which he builds up details and about the relationship between physical features and information about occupation.

He very rarely condemns his characters outright. He is much more likely to use **irony** to encourage the reader to question the integrity of the individual pilgrims. For instance, consider the Prioress who has such perfect table manners. The first detail Chaucer tells us about this nun is:

> **KEYWORD**
>
> Irony: in simple terms, an expression of meaning in language which seems to suggest the opposite. Irony has become a dominant mode in English culture and often allows the reader to see what fictional characters cannot. The basis of satire.

That of hir smylyng was ful symple and coy

That her smiling was very unaffected and quiet

This sounds fairly charming and inoffensive. It is only later that the reader pauses to wonder whether this isn't rather a strange piece of information with which to begin a description of a holy woman. Similarly, the fact that her greatest pleasure is in good manners then begins to seem curious. It is more reassuring to know that:

She was so charitable and so pitous

She was so charitable and so compassionate

But the next lines undercut her compassion:

She wolde wepe, if that she saugh a mous
Kaught in a trappe, if it were deed or bledde.

*She would weep if she saw a mouse
Caught in a trap, if it was dead or bleeding.*

We need to read this description against the ideal of a prioress, a woman who has devoted her life to the service of God, and whose duty is to care for all Christian souls. If we do this, then the gentle irony with which Chaucer describes *his* Prioress becomes obvious. He does not condemn her outright, he just suggests to the audience, through the details he chooses, that the things she considers important are not appropriate for a woman in her position. If she wasn't a prioress she may well be a very good person. However, in his investigation of the way society works, Chaucer is suggesting that there is a problem - if prioresses are worried only about mice, then who has compassion for mankind?

'I am dronke – I know it by my soun'

Another of Chaucer's techniques of characterization is to tell the reader whose opinion he is presenting. For instance, he says of the Pardoner's lack of a hood: 'Hym thoughte he rood [rode] al of the newe jet [fashion]' – he thought he looked dashing and fashionable on his horse. Knowing this is what *he* thought immediately makes the reader wonder what everyone else thought …

When The Prologue is ended, Chaucer has managed to describe a collection of people who are individualized enough to be memorable. But he has also made them typical, representative enough for their virtues and vices to have a wider significance than this particular pilgrimage to Canterbury. You can read more about this in Chapter 5.

THE CANTERBURY TALES

There are 24 tales altogether, written between 1388 and Chaucer's death in 1400. The work was never finished, however, as each pilgrim was supposed to tell four tales in all according to the plan set out by the host at the start of the journey. There is also a good deal of uncertainty about how the tales relate to one another. Some of the tales are linked together with passages of dialogue where the pilgrims comment on the tale they have just heard and the host asks the next person to begin his or her story. These sections remind the reader of the fictional pilgrimage during which the stories are being told, providing a frame into which they slot.

There are ten 'fragments', or groups within which the tales are linked together in this way and, although some scholars have seen links between the fragments themselves, the order in which they should be read is the subject of considerable debate.

The Knight – teller of the first tale

The one thing we can be certain about is who tells the first tale. The importance of this is made clear as the pilgrims leave London. Their host stops them and tells them:

> Now draweth cut, er that we ferrer twynne;
> He which that hath the shorteste shal bigynne.

> *Now draw lots before we depart any further;*
> *Whoever has the shortest shall begin.*

When all the pilgrims have drawn their lots, Chaucer tells us,

> Were it by aventure, or sort, or cas,
> The sothe is this: the cut fil to the Knyght,
> Of which ful blithe and glad was every wyght

> *By chance, luck or destiny,*
> *The truth is this: the cut fell to the Knight,*
> *Of which everyone was happy and glad*

What a piece of luck – the most important man on the pilgrimage, their highest status companion, draws the short straw! There would seem to be a certain amount of irony in Chaucer's description of this beginning as luck, but in any case the tale telling begins with great decorum.

What type of tale does the Knight tell?

The tale the Knight tells is a considerably expanded and altered adaptation of a well-known story which is also told by Boccaccio.

Chaucer's version concentrates on the activities of two young knights called Palamon and Arcite who are imprisoned after a battle. From their prison window they see a lady in the garden below. She is fairer to look at 'Than is the lylie [lily] upon his stalke grene'; they both fall in love with her, and compete to win her for themselves.

This story is a **romance**. Romance was one of the most important literary forms in Chaucer's day, and had been for nearly two centuries. The typical romance is set in a foreign place in a far away time, and the events of the story are controlled by chance encounters and unusual happenings. The heroes and heroines of romance are epitomes of aristocratic conduct,

KEYWORD

Romance: a narrative of courtly and chivalrous behaviour, usually involving a quest and often containing supernatural elements.

and their behaviour demonstrates how life *might be* if everyone was as virtuous as they were, rather than how life actually *is*. The style of a romance is elaborate and the pace at which the story is told is leisurely and unhurried.

Take this example of love at first sight. Whilst Palamon is pacing in his cell, crying 'Alas' that he was ever born, he sees Emily:

> And so bifel, by adventure or cas,
> That thurgh a wyndow, thikke of many a barre
> Of iren greet and square as any sparre,
> He cast his eye upon Emelya,
> And therwithal he bleynte and cride, 'A!'
> As though he stongen were unto the herte.

> *And so it happened, by chance or accident,*
> *That through a window, thickly set with many bars*
> *Of iron great and thick as a wooden beam,*
> *He cast his eye on Emily,*
> *And with that he turned pale and cried 'Ah!'*
> *As though he had been pierced to the heart.*

You can see in this passage the emphasis on the chance nature of the knight's love, the considerable length of the description, and the power of just seeing the remote and inaccessible beloved. These features are all typical of a romance. So the Knight tells just the kind of story which everyone expected him to tell. It is a romance full of knights and their ladies and extols the virtues of the knightly class: their moral codes and the behaviour which these lead to.

When he has finished, everyone says it was 'a noble storie', especially 'the gentils everichon'. This is a tale which impresses the whole company, but especially the gentlefolk – those who share the same ideals as the Knight (the subject matter which he chooses), and who enjoy and are familiar with the kind of tale he tells (romance as a form which stories take).

Who wins the fight to go next?

The host, who had probably made sure that proper decorum was followed when the Knight drew the short straw, then asks the Monk 'to quite with the Knyghtes tale', meaning to repay it, or to match it with one of his own. However, before the Monk can accept, the Miller, who is drunk, swears that he has the perfect tale to 'quite' the Knight's.

'She wolde wepe, if that she saugn a mous Kaught in a trappe, if it were deed or bledde'

The argument which follows, the first to break out on the pilgrimage, is all about social status. Harry Bailey tells the Miller that 'Som bettre man shal telle us first another': someone who is of higher status than he is. Other pilgrims object to the subject matter of the tale which the Miller proposes – a story about a carpenter who is deceived by the clerk who sleeps with his wife. The Reeve tells him to 'Stynt thy clappe!', as it is a sin to defame a man, or to slander wives.

What kind of tale does the Miller tell?

The tale which the Miller insists on telling is one of sex, humour, and a certain amount of carefully directed violence involving a piece of hot iron! It is a type of tale called a **fabliau**, which originated in France in the thirteenth century. These are stories set in recognizably familiar places, about the often obscene antics of lower or middling status people. They are not realistic, as you'll see when you read what the Miller said, because the goings on are just as far-fetched as those of romance but in a different way. The Reeve's worries about slander show that the difference is one of **realism** – unlike romances, fabliaux are made to look real, like a soap opera today, perhaps.

The heroes in fabliaux are young and very clever, but they are the kind of people who have very little power in the real-life world outside the story – young wives and young clerks for instance. Their victims are often the virtuous in society, so the genre as a whole has a tendency to be **subversive**.

The style is bold and simple. Compare this extract to the one from the Knight's Tale. Nicholas, finally alone with the carpenter's young wife,

… heeld hire harde by the haunchebones,
And seyde, 'Lemman, love me al atones,
Or I wol dyen, also God me save!'

… held her hard by the thighs,
And said, 'Sweetheart, love me immediately,
Or I will die, God save me!'

Although he too is experiencing his beloved for the first time, Nicholas's sentiments are rather different from those of Palamon the knight. The physicality of the situation and Nicholas's practical way of dealing with his desire are a huge contrast to the languishing, imprisoned courtly lover of romance. In style, emotion and even length, the two passages contrast each other sharply.

Why are the two tales so different?
The two types of story, the Knight's romance and the Miller's fabliau, are in many ways opposites of one another, just as their tellers are. For this reason the tale of Alison and her lover Nicholas really does 'quite' that of Palamon and Arcite: the idealized morality of the romance is answered by the insatiable sexuality of the fabliau.

So different kinds of pilgrims are expected to tell different kinds of tales – not only with different subject matter, but in different literary genres. Chaucer isn't trying to tell us that millers only knew or enjoyed dirty stories, or that knights didn't like them at all, but he is using differences in the status of his pilgrims as a motivation for telling a variety of kinds of story in *The Canterbury Tales*.

The opposition between the Knight's Tale and the Miller's is a source of comedy, but it also opens up a debate about literary form and moral standards which you can read more about in the next chapter on Major Themes. These two tales are only examples – many other tales are influenced by the fabliau tradition, such as the Reeve's, the Cook's, the Friar's and the Merchant's. There are other romances, too, such as the Wife of Bath's, the Franklin's, the Man of Law's and the Squire's. In addition, there are tales influenced by popular minstrelsy; miracles of the Virgin; literary confessions; moralizing allegories; saints' lives; sermons; and beast fables. There is an enormous richness and variety of subject matter, narrative form and poetic style.

Chaucer always develops the genre he is writing in – he never writes a standard, conventional tale, and he often combines genres within the same tale. For instance, the Franklin's Tale is a romance, but it is also an exemplary tale, which demonstrates strength of character as individuals are made to keep their word through the severest tests.

CHAUCER'S OTHER WORKS

Chaucer wrote many other long and short poems and suggestions for further reading are given in Chapter 8. Here are two poems which are linked thematically to some of the issues raised in *The Canterbury Tales* which offer a useful starting place to start approaching his other works.

Troilus and Criseyde

Troilus and Criseyde was written between 1381 and 1386, when Chaucer had already developed a reputation at Court as a poet of courtly love. He was writing it around the time that he wrote the Knight's Tale, and before he started on *The Canterbury Tales* as a whole. It is the only one of his long poems which he completely finished and gave structure and shape to, dividing it into five books and giving it a proper ending.

The story is set in the Trojan Wars, a popular topic for medieval writers. They tell the history of the conflict in its entirely, or as a series of numerous different kinds of tale grouped around the same central event. It was of particular interest in Chaucer's period because a history of Britain written by Geoffrey of Monmouth had suggested that Britain was founded by the Trojan hero Brut. There was even a proposal that London should be renamed 'Troynovant', or new Troy, in the 1380s.

A wartime love story

Rather than a story of battles and heroism, Chaucer tells the tale of the love between Troilus, who is the son of King Priam of Troy, and

Criseyde who is the daughter of a priest of Troy called Calchas. Calchas foresees the fall of the great city in the future and goes over to the Greek side, leaving his daughter behind.

Troilus observes Criseyde from afar and falls in love instantly: 'O mercy, God' he says as he spies her in the crowd in a temple, and 'Therwith his herte [be]gan to sprede and rise'. He is helped in his wooing by Pandarus, Criseyde's uncle, who acts as a go-between and brings the couple together. However, an exchange of prisoners is arranged between the two sides in the war, and Criseyde is part of the bargain. She is sent to the Greek camp, where Diomedes, a noble warrior from the other side, woos and finally wins her.

Boccaccio's story, on which this poem is based, recounts the tragedy of the betrayal which Troilus suffers at the hands of Criseyde. But Chaucer's extended and completely altered version gives a great deal more space to the wooing and the love affair between them: it is about how Troilus's 'aventures fellen/ Fro wo to wele, and after out of joie' – from woe to happiness and then out of bliss again. It is very funny in places, opening with the shock which Troilus feels as a life-long scoffer about love and a man who mocks all his friends when they fall in love with women. 'O veray [true] fooles, nyce [foolish] and blynde be ye', he says to the lovesick knights and ladies. After one look at Criseyde, however, he is overtaken with melancholy, crying a thousand times:

> 'My dere herte, allas, myn hele and hewe
> And lif is lost, but ye wol on me rewe!'

> *'My dear heart, alas, my health and colour*
> *And life is lost, unless you have pity on me!'*

The Legend of Good Women
The Legend of Good Women was written around 1386–7, about the same time as Chaucer was writing *The Canterbury Tales*, and a few years after he had finished Troilus and Criseyde.

The prologue to this work, like that of *The Canterbury Tales,* begins in spring, in 'the joly tyme of May,/ Whan that I here the smale foules [birds] synge,/ And that the floures gynne [begin] for to sprynge'. The poet falls asleep, and the scene which follows is a wonderful example of a popular medieval

KEYWORD

Dream vision: a device in medieval writing where the narrator goes to sleep and 'dreams' the work.

form of writing called the **dream vision**. The poet dreams that he is lying in a spring meadow when he sees the god of love coming towards him with his queen, a beautiful woman who looks like a daisy.

Chaucer gets into trouble with love

The god spies him watching and asks him, 'What dost thow her [here]/ In my presence, and that so boldely?' He is not pleased to see Chaucer, saying that he would rather 'A worm to comen in my syght than thow'.

It transpires that, unfortunately for Chaucer, Love has heard of him, and the reason for this hostility is the kind of poetry which Chaucer has been writing:

> Thow art my mortal fo and me werreyest,
> And of myne olde servauntes thow mysseyest,
> And hynderest hem with thy translacyoun,
> And lettest folk to han devocyoun
> To serven me, and holdest it folye
> To truste on me.

> *You are my mortal foe and wage war upon me,*
> *And you slander my old servants,*
> *And hinder them with your translation [of poems],*
> *And obstruct people from paying serious attention*
> *To serving me, and consider it folly*
> *To trust me.*

Chaucer meets his match

Love says Chaucer cannot deny this as it is there for everyone to see 'in pleyn text' – in his translation of the *Romance of the Rose*. He also demands:

> Hast thow nat mad in Englysh ek the bok
> How that Crisseyde Troylus forsook,
> In shewynge how that wemen han don mis?

> *Did you not also write the book in English*
> *[Which tells] how Criseyde forsook Troilus,*
> *In showing how women have done wrong?*

Chaucer defends himself by saying that:

> … it was myn entente
> To forthere trouthe in love and it cheryce,
> And to be war fro falsnesse and fro vice
> By swich ensaumple

... it was my intention
To further truth in love and cherish it
And to be warned from falseness and from vice
By such an example

He had intended, by telling stories like that of *Troilus and Criseyde*, to provide a cautionary tale. Although Chaucer claims that this is to the greater glory of true love, he still receives a penance. He is to make:

… a glorious legende
Of goode women, maydenes and wyves …
And telle of false men that [t]hem betrayen [betrayed]

The rest of the poem is taken up with his response to this task, nine tales of classical heroines such as Cleopatra, Dido and Ariadne. The dream vision provides a framework for the different stories in a similar way to the idea of pilgrimage and the conversations between the pilgrims in *The Canterbury Tales*.

✳ ✳ ✳ *SUMMARY* ✳ ✳ ✳

● Medieval poets often retell older tales.

● Chaucer's pilgrims are individualized types.

● *The Canterbury Tales* are very varied in subject matter, style and genre.

● Chaucer makes the story of *Troilus and Criseyde* into a love story as well as a tale of betrayal.

● Chaucer presents *The Legend of Good Women* as his own punishment for slandering women!

5 Major themes

This chapter discusses the ways in which Chaucer writes about chivalry and romance; what he tells his readers about the relations between the sexes; and the importance of society and community in his poetry. These three topics could be considered to be themes of Chaucer's writing. But what is a theme?

In the broadest sense we can think of a theme as a topic which crops up repeatedly in an author's work. There might be different reasons for this recurrence. The author might be interested personally in the ideas; the genre in which the work is written might *usually* deal with such topics; or the society of which the author is a part might be particularly concerned with them. For instance, chivalry is a feature of romance narratives and we can tell that relations between the sexes and the nature of community are issues of general social concern because other writers, contemporary with Chaucer, also discuss these topics.

These are by no means the only issues which are raised in Chaucer's work, but they are some of the most prominent. If you are interested in pursuing other aspects which link the poems, Chapter 8 will offer some suggestions.

CHIVALRY AND ROMANCE

You have already read about the Knight's tale in *The Canterbury Tales*, so you know that romance was a very popular genre in Chaucer's time. Knights were able to win honour in great tournaments and the Crusades were still taking place. English knights were travelling to non-Christian lands when Christians were in danger or under attack, and they were going to war to relieve occupied territories. Some less principled bands of knights, however, were starting to act as mercenaries – offering their military services to the highest bidder with scant regard for the holiness of the war.

What kind of world do romances show the reader?

So romance writing was doing two things at once when Chaucer was producing his poems. It was reflecting some of the activities undertaken by the social elite of England, showing recognizable scenes and actions, but it was also giving a picture of a model of behaviour which was not necessarily a picture of how things were really being done: writing romances meant putting forward the ideals of chivalry, the epitome of aristocratic behaviour.

The basic principles of chivalry were that a knight should show courage and that he should demonstrate honour – especially the mercy which he would show to an opponent. Behaving in a chivalric fashion also meant displaying elaborate and complicated manners – there were special ways of conducting every kind of social situation, and getting them wrong brought shame upon everybody concerned. These manners were important because they were moralized – they became a way of judging how virtuous a person was by the way he or she acted.

For this reason, the Wife of Bath's Tale ends with a double transformation. The knight is given the choice between a wife who is ugly and faithful or beautiful and potentially unfaithful. He chooses faithfulness and is rewarded for this by having the best of both worlds – she becomes beautiful as well. But the knight himself is also transformed in the process. At the start of the tale he is a gentleman in the sense that he is high born, but his actions are anything but gentle – he rapes a young noblewoman. By the end of the tale he has learned his lesson and has realized that true gentility lies in what you do rather than in what you are. The tale is a triumph of the moral virtues of chivalry.

What are the rules of courtly love?

One of the most complex aspects of chivalric behaviour was courtly love. Here the knight's erotic impulses were made virtuous by being spiritualized. Instead of lusting after his lady and hoping for a physical relationship with her, he idolizes and idealizes her, suffering agonies of mind and body for his devotion. As she is often already married to someone else, the most he can hope for is that he will remain devoted to her, and that his devotion will improve him and make him a better person.

The Knight's Tale gives Chaucer the opportunity to demonstrate the tortures of love. As we have already seen in the previous chapter, the knights first catch sight of Emelye on a May morning:

> Yclothed was she fressh, for to devyse …
> And in the gardyn, at the sonne upriste,
> She walketh up and doun, and as hire liste
> She gadereth floures, party white and rede

> *She was clothed freshly, for to tell …*
> *And in the garden at sunrise,*
> *She walks up and down, and as she pleased*
> *She gathers flower, part white and part red*

She is strolling freely (as hire liste), gathering flowers on a spring day. They are looking at her 'thurgh a wyndow, thickke of many a barre/ Of iren' – through the iron bars of their prison in a tower. Chaucer uses the contrast between the garden and the tower to make a point about the pains which their love causes them – it is like being a prisoner, unable to move about freely, doomed to see your beloved but never to have any contact with her.

Chaucer mocks the conventions of courtly love

In other tales, however, Chaucer mocks the whole idea of courtly love. In the Miller's Tale the young and beautiful Alison, wife of the old carpenter John, is courted by two men. One is the clever and witty Nicholas who is a student lodging in their house, the other is the parish clerk, Absolon. Chaucer describes Absolon in terms appropriate for a courtly lover. He takes great pains over his appearance:

Crul was his heer, and as the gold it shoon,
And strouted as a fanne large and brode…
His rode was reed, his eyen greye as goos.
With Poules wyndow corven on his shoos

Curled was his hair, and as the gold it shone
And stretched out like a fan large and broad…
His complexion was red, his eyes grey as a goose
With holes cut in his shoes like a stained glass window
[Literally with Paul's window carved on his shoes]

He also has very 'noble' manners. He is 'somdeel squaymous' [a little squeamish] 'Of fartyng'! At night, Chaucer tells us, he stays awake 'for the sake of love', takes his cithern [a kind of lute] and stands under Alison's window:

He syngeth in his voys gentil and smal,
'Now, deere lady, if thy wille be,
I praye yow that ye wole rewe on me,'
Ful wel acordaunt to his gyternynge.

He sings in his voice gentle and high,
'Now, dear lady, if your will be,
I pray you have mercy on me,'
In harmony with his cithern playing.

In the Knight's Tale this would be entirely appropriate behaviour, and we wouldn't find ourselves laughing. It is because he's a parish clerk in a fabliau, rather than a knight in a romance, and because he's standing in a street in the town rather than a garden of a castle, that the scene is so funny. You can immediately guess from the description of Absolon that it is Nicholas who gets the girl!

So Chaucer uses the language, the actions and the images of chivalric romance traditionally in the Knight's Tale, and then in completely the wrong setting to comic effect in the Miller's Tale. If the audience didn't understand the conventions of romance, they wouldn't find Absolon's behaviour nearly so funny.

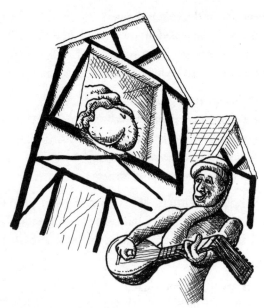

'He syngeth in his voys gentil and small'

RELATIONS BETWEEN THE SEXES

In Chaucer's time, as is the case today, there were many different ways of thinking about and writing about men and women. Ideas about women were heavily influenced by the two most important women in medieval life – Eve and the Virgin Mary.

These two were the epitome of the best and the worst aspects of female nature. One disobeyed God in the Garden of Eden and condemned mankind to suffering and death; the other gave birth to Jesus, the Son of God, whose death saved mankind from eternal damnation. Their lives were offered as a warning and a role model respectively to women in sermons, in art, and in the writings of learned churchmen.

Saints

The principles of courtly love, as we've already seen, entailed a very positive attitude towards women. Women were spiritually superior to men and had the power to improve them morally. Men, when they pledged allegiance to a woman as their lover, did so to a woman whom they thought of as perfect – as the epitome of all the best aspects of female nature. So there are clear connections between courtly love and the worship of the Virgin Mary – both involve idealizing and idolizing women.

Several of the stories in *The Canterbury Tales* present women in this positive light. The Clerk tells a tale about a poor woman called Grisilde who is chosen by Walter, the lord of the land, to be his wife. Walter takes her from her father's house and dresses her in fine clothes.The story is about the tests to which he subjects her in order to prove her obedience to him. He takes away her children and sends her back to her cottage stripped of her fine clothes, but at every turn she obeys him unquestioningly, proving her moral strength until she is eventually returned to her rightful position.

It is a very hard and cruel lesson but the Clerk tells this tale as a moral exemplum – an allegory of the obedience human beings should show to God – rather than as a realistic story of the way husbands and wives should behave towards each other. He says:

> This storie is seyd nat for that wyves sholde
> Folwen Grisilde as in humylite
> For it were inportable, though they woulde,
> But for that every wight, in his degree,
> Sholde be constant in adversitee.

> *This story isn't told with the intention that wives should*
> *Follow Grisilde in humility*
> *Because it would be intollerable if they would,*
> *But so that every person, in his degree,*
> *Should be constant in adversity*

So the first thing to be said about the portrayal of the relationship between the sexes in Chaucer's work is that we need to be aware of the kind of tale we're being told. Tales like the Clerk's deal with 'model' women, presenting the traits of idealized womanhood in order to make a point about how we would all behave if we were perfect. If we respond to characters like Grisilde and Walter as though they were realistic portrayals of the everyday behaviour of husbands and wives then we are missing the point. We need to understand *what* is being said in relation to *where* it is being said.

Sinners

In contrast to this positive view of women there was a considerable amount of writing about 'bad women' in the medieval period. Taking Eve as their subject, many monastic writers waxed lyrical about the essential evil of women's weakness and blamed them for the state of the world. They had a particular axe to grind – the monastic life was a celibate one, and these men were reacting towards women partly as representatives of the world which they had renounced to concentrate on spiritual matters. Relations with women were the antithesis of monastic life and this made some monks very hostile towards them and towards the whole institution of marriage.

One of the loudest spoken was St Jerome, who produced the Vulgate Bible. In his *Epistle against Jovinian* he builds biblical quotes into an anti-feminist diatribe:

> 'A continual dropping on a wintry day' turns a man out of doors, and so will a contentious woman drive a man from his own house. She floods his house with her constant nagging and daily chatter, and ousts him from his own home, that is, the Church.

From Miller, *Chaucer: Sources and Backgrounds* (Oxford University Press, 1977) p. 427.

This type of writing, which was very familiar to Chaucer and his contemporaries, presents an image of women as naturally deceitful, unduly emotional, and given to constant nattering.

What did the Wife of Bath think about 'bad women'?

It is just this kind of writing which makes the Wife of Bath, Chaucer's most famous spokesperson on this subject, so very cross. 'No woman' she says, 'of no clerk is preysed': clerks will never praise women because they are biased by their celibate lives, whereas, 'if wommen hadde writen stories…They wolde han writen of men moore wikkednesse/ Than al the mark of Adam may redresse' – women could tell stories of more wicked things done by men than all the male sex could make amends for.

The Wife understands why such stories are told about women and goes about to disprove them in the long prologue to her tale. This is written as a kind of sermon – Chaucer uses direct questions to the audience and cries of frustration to animate her argument. She, like St Jerome, weighs all the evidence of the Bible, finding that Christ did not insist on virginity, and that St Paul only advised it, rather than commanding it. But she adds one other ingredient, the word with which she opens her prologue, 'experience'.

Marriage to her five husbands provides the Wife with a good deal of material for her debate! She sets the evidence of experience against that of 'authority', here meaning written authority – the evidence of books written by men. The culmination of her attempts to find a form of marriage which is acceptable to both partners comes as a result of an incident with a 'Book of Wicked Wives' which her fifth husband Jankyn owns.

Jankyn is a scholar, and his book gathers together the writings of many other scholars and respected authors on the subject of the evils carried out by women through the ages. When the Wife has finally had enough of the stories he reads to her from it, she rips out the pages and a fight ensues during which he nearly kills her. Taking advantage of his fear that she is dead and his remorse, she engineers an agreement whereby she takes control of the marriage – 'He yaf [gave] me al the bridel in myn hond [hand]' – and he burns the hated book. From this moment on they 'hadden never debaat', and they were faithful and kind to one another. She claims to have solved the riddle of perfect marital harmony.

The Wife of Bath is a lively and endearing character – we just can't help but like her. In order to understand what we're being told as readers about the relationship between men and women, however, we must be clear about the way in which Chaucer constructs her character. Part of the joke here is that the Wife is a perfect example of all the faults of which she tells us women are accused. She clearly talks too much – the length of the prologue proves that! – and she is, in her own way, deceitful. She tricks Jankyn into giving up his authority over their marriage.

Reading the prologue could have been rather dull – after all it is basically a debate about clerical attitudes towards women. However, the Wife is so full of righteous indignation and interprets the Bible in such a quirky and unexpected way in the light of her own experience, that the passage is instead very funny, and a character who Chaucer puts together from scraps of insults about the female sex becomes memorably individualized.

What did Chaucer think about men and women?
Chaucer offers the reader many other representations of men and women in several of his shorter poems, but also in the longer works. As you have already seen in the Prologue to *The Legend of Good Women*, he translated and rewrote many famous stories about human relationships. If we want to establish what Chaucer thought, about women for instance, we would need to read all of these poems. That said, this still might not present us with an answer, as there is no one consistent view being presented which we can identify as the author's own.

What kind of debates take place about men and women?
Many of Chaucer's poems take up a moral standpoint on the relationship between men and women, but some of the stories within *The Canterbury Tales* go further than just presenting tales on the same

theme. The Wife of Bath's prologue, for instance, is clearly intended to influence the way we read the tale itself, with its central question 'What thyng is it that wommen moost desiren'. There are also clear links between the Wife's story and those of other pilgrims.

The Merchant's Tale, for instance, also contains a debate about marriage in which the Wife is actually cited as an authority. The Clerk's Tale about the patience of Grisilde is another example. At the end of the story, the Clerk makes it clear that he is aware of the opinion of the Wife of Bath, not least about clerks and their tales of women! Having said that it is hard to find in any town nowadays 'Grisildis thre or two', he says he will lighten the mood by singing a song, 'for the Wyves love of Bathe [for the love of the Wife of Bath] Whos lyf and al hire secte God mayntene'. The fact that he is trying to lighten the mood here and avoid confrontation suggests a level of tension between the pilgrims which makes readers focus on the opposing view points which might give rise to it.

This gives the ideas presented in the different tales a coherence, and clearly suggests to readers that they should think about the different opinions being offered in relation to one another. Because the pilgrims are debating this matter between themselves readers, too, should approach them as a debate about the relationships between men and women in marriage.

Of course this doesn't only happen in *The Canterbury Tales*. Even between Chaucer's poems there is debate, and the Prologue to *The Legend of Good Women* makes this very clear. Chaucer is obviously very self-concious about the kind of stories he is telling about human relationships, and he appears, even if only for the sake of comic effect, to be interested in maintaining some kind of balance between 'good' and 'bad' women.

We are not told what to think – the poems are not a moralized lesson for readers to learn about how they should or should not behave. There *are* lessons to be learned, but we are able to decide for ourselves what those might be through the open-ended debate which Chaucer constructs between a series of stories which have themes in common with one another. This aspect of debate makes marriage and gender a different kind of theme from chivalry and romance. It is presented with a degree of self-consciousness which has implications for the form and structure of the poems.

SOCIETY AND COMMUNITY

What do different tales tell us about society?

When the Miller insists on telling his tale after the Knight's, he upsets the hierarchical ordering of the tales. He purposefully ensures that they will not be organized according to the social status of the tellers. By making him intervene in this way, Chaucer makes it possible to open debates on various themes, because to hear a knight talking about the relationship between the sexes doesn't constitute a debate, it is only when the same issue is seen from several different perspectives that the reader begins to appreciate how complicated it is, and to think about whether there can be one definitive answer which will hold true for a whole society.

So a debate in which those of a variety of social levels are engaged is one way of discussing community – of looking at how it operates through how it deliberates important issues. You can read more about the conclusion to such debates in the next chapter

Estates satire allows Chaucer to comment on society

The General Prologue to *The Canterbury Tales* indicates the traditional division of society into three estates – those who fight, those who pray, and those who work. Medieval social theory saw this as producing an ideal harmony through the division of labour, but it worked only if all discharged their responsibilities fully and all were content with their lot. The Black Death had shaken this ideal because there were not enough labourers to do all the work; Lollardy had highlighted abuses within the Church which suggested that those who prayed were not devoting themselves to a sacred life; and, as you will read in the chapter after, the role of the knightly classes in defending the Christian faith was also coming under attack.

Chaucer's often ironic depiction of the pilgrims signals some of the tensions which were threatening this stable world view. If we see the group as a whole as in some way symbolic of his contemporary society, then there are clearly serious problems.

Occupational satire also permits comment

In addition to the theory of the three estates, Chaucer uses the individual occupations of the pilgrims to make a point about society. He does this by stressing the employment of the characters in the tales the pilgrims tell. For instance, the Reeve's Tale is taken from a French fabliau, but Chaucer alters this source to make the story interact with the preceding Miller's Tale. In the Reeve's cynical and nasty story, a thieving miller is cuckolded and beaten. In addition, the Friar's Tale is about a corrupt sumner and the Sumner's Tale is, of course, about a hypocritical friar.

These connections are mainly comic, but they do provide a further way of considering the stereotypes of estates literature in relation to the individualized characters telling the tales. This offers another level of interaction between ideal and reality which invites us to query the accuracy of the former and to consider the implications of what we find acceptable for society as a whole.

This also happens to a certain extent within The General Prologue itself. For instance, Chaucer portrays the Parson as one of the rare wholly admirable pilgrims: we are told that he goes to great lengths to care for his congregation and that he doesn't suffer from any of the vices traditionally associated with parsons. Later on we are told that the Pardoner gets more money in a day than a parson gets in two months. The connection between this non-specific parson, to whom the Pardoner is compared, and the particular Parson whom we admire, invites us to judge the Pardoner through his distortion of the way a moral society ought to function.

Nobility offers a further method of division

In addition to dividing society by estate and by occupation, Chaucer also investigates the difference between those who are 'gentil' and those who are not in *The Canterbury Tales*. This concept is questioned in many different ways, not least in the repeated and increasingly ironic use of the word 'gentle' as a description of the pilgrims in The General Prologue.

The Wife of Bath's Tale, as we have already seen, also comments on what it means to be gentle. The high-born knight who rapes the girl at the start of the tale eventually learns that being gentle is a question of actions as well as birth. The romances in general in *The Canterbury Tales*, with their emphasis on being able to tell a hero by his behaviour, by the chivalrous codes which he follows, contain a great deal of information on the connections between gentle birth and being a gentleman.

✳ ✳ ✳ *SUMMARY* ✳ ✳ ✳

● Chivalry is a feature of the romance genre, and its conventions can be manipulated to comic effect.

● We need to understand the portrayal of different themes in relation to the kind of tale in which they appear.

● Although there's no one view which we can identify as Chaucer's, there is self-conscious debate.

● Chaucer examines a variety of different ways of structuring society.

The contemporary literary scene

BOOKS AND READING IN CHAUCER'S TIME

When you bought this book you probably just picked it up off the shelf, paid for it and took it home. Maybe you didn't even leave the house with the intention of buying it; you certainly didn't enter into lengthy and complex negotiations with the bookseller to commission your copy of it. And you would probably be surprised if you looked at another copy and found that this chapter was missing!

In order to understand how Chaucer's earliest readers appreciated his work, it is necessary to know something about their attitudes towards books and reading in general. When Chaucer was writing his poetry, making a book was a complex and laborious process. Each new copy had to be individually produced by a scribe.

How were books made?

Before a scribe could begin to write, he had to have something to write *on*. The skins of animals were treated in a lime solution to remove the hair from the surface. Then they were repeatedly soaked and stretched flat, degreased and bleached, until a thin, smooth, and long-lasting surface had been created which could be written on. Called parchment, this was then cut into shapes suitable for making a book.

Scribes prepared inks from compounds of carbon, or from a powder made from the galls which grow on oak trees. When the text had been written onto the pages, rubricators (literally people who painted in red letters) then added titles, headings, or initial letters to draw attention to particular parts of the text. If the book was to be a very elaborate one, illuminators would then decorate it with images.

Books were beautiful and expensive objects

Books were beautiful just as objects in themselves, and they were also very expensive indeed to produce. Chaucer says that the Clerk of

Oxford who is on the pilgrimage would rather have 'twenty bookes, clad in blak or reed' than rich robes or a fiddle. Scholars estimate that such a library would have cost him about 60 times his annual income. The 'Book of Wikked Wyves' from which the Wife of Bath rips some of the pages would have been worth several hundred pounds – so you can see why it made her husband so cross!

Jankyn was also cross because books contained authoritative knowledge: he thought that his one *proved* that men are superior to women. This status came from their compilation out of quotations from other texts. This **intertextuality** depersonalized knowledge – it wasn't seen as *interpretation* so much as *truth*, because it was objectively free of the intervention of an author. Jankyn's book, like many others, drew considerable authority from the epitome of the sacred, untouchable book, the one which offered knowledge of God – the Bible.

KEYWORD

Intertextuality: a relationship between texts where the language, themes, images or ideas of one text are alluded to in another.

Very few people owned books outside the institutions of learning (universities and monasteries) in the fourteenth-century. Even people renowned for collecting books didn't have very many by modern standards. Richard de Bury, the fourteenth-century Bishop of Durham and tutor to the young Edward III, probably had the most - about 1,500 volumes – but he was very unusual indeed.

How did scribes copy books?

As the scribe copied a book, he might include his comments on the text in the margins. Readers of the copy might add to these, sometimes filling the whole page with their interpretation of the author's meaning. The important point here is that the distinctions with which we are so familiar between the author, the person who produces the book, and the reader, aren't really relevant to the medieval production of books. Scribes added to what they copied, and sometimes they left out bits they thought were irrelevant. This makes them interested readers and also, in a way, authors too. So it is no use looking for an 'accurate' text of *The Canterbury Tales* as Chaucer intended it, instead we have to think about the aspects of the text which were important to writers and readers of Chaucer in the first centuries after he was writing.

What are the manuscripts of Chaucer's work like?

No text of *The Canterbury Tales* written in Chaucer's own hand survives. In fact there are no fourteenth-century manuscripts of Chaucer's work – the earliest copies we have come from the fifteenth century. There are 82 manuscripts – a huge number compared to the existing copies of other poems.

The manuscripts of *The Canterbury Tales* are remarkable because there are so many of them from all over the country, not just London, and because they are of a wide variety of qualities, suggesting lots of different kinds of readers. Two of them, copied in the first decade of the fifteenth century by the same scribe, are thought to be the best. They are called the Hengwrt and the Ellesmere manuscripts, and most modern editions of the poem are based on them.

MEDIEVAL READING

This book began by suggesting that you read slowly. That advice wasn't necessary only because the language is difficult, the whole *idea* of reading in the medieval period was very different from our own. Reading Chaucer was originally a very active process and readers had to work very hard.

Memory power

Copying on parchment wasn't the only way of reproducing texts. Richard de Bury, the man with the huge library, depended on a whole army of clerks to read new religious arguments from the continent and bring them back to him in their memories. He describes these men as being like keen hunters after rabbits. The books of Paris and Athens, he says, 'while they lie quietly…are moved, while holding their own places they are borne everywhere in the minds of their listeners'.

Because we live in a literate society we have come to associate not being able to read with a lack of intelligence. However, we have, in fact lost the ability to remember things in the ways which were possible in the medieval period – whole books for instance. In Chaucer's time, very few people could read, and that meant that they could remember vast amounts of information without the need to write it down. Most information was exchanged orally and a great deal of learning and teaching went on without the need for pens, paper, or books.

Memory was an art. If you were a scholar, lawyer or merchant you might want to train your memory with the aid of various treatises which were being produced from the thirteenth to the fifteenth centuries. There were lots of interesting metaphors for memory. It was described as valuable coins to be laid away for the future in the memory chest, or as the flowers of reading to be gathered by readers as bees gather nectar. Having your memory jogged was compared to hooking a fish and drawing it out through the waters of your mind.

This is important because Chaucer's poetry may well have been read to its original audience. This might explain the form it takes – the use of minute description and particular details which help to build up an image of the people and things he is describing which listeners can easily imagine and remember.

What do you do with what you remember?
In every case what you remembered was valuable (the phrase 'pearls of wisdom' was being used in Chaucer's time), and as with money or nectar, you can *make* something from what you remember. So, when you read a book, first you memorize what you find there so that you can carry it with you wherever you go. Later, you can retrieve this information, and the metaphor which is used for this process is chewing the cud, like a cow. Medieval monks were told to *murmur*, to mouth the words under their breath as they thought about what they had read, and they thought this sounded like a regurgitating cow!

'Remember, remember …'

The point of this ruminative meditation was to internalize reading completely in a moral sense. It is a transformative process whereby first the reader admires the virtues which are shown in the text, and then changes his or her own life and thought to imitate them. We need to think about this moral aspect as one way of reading Chaucer's work.

Reading was a serious business – but books were fun

Just because reading has a serious moral intention, we shouldn't think that medieval books didn't allow you to have a sense of humour. In fact they often used humour as a way of making readers remember, making them look hard at the text. Look in the margins of expensive illustrated books and you will see witty images, sometimes even scandalous ones! This even applies to the Bible. The beautifully illustrated Book of Kells begins St Mathew's Gospel with a page which says 'Christi hic generatio', or 'This is how Christ was born'. Within the enormous patterned letters of the word 'Christ' are two cats, several mice who are eating a communion wafer, and a black otter eating a salmon.

Chaucer employs the same kind of strategy – by making us laugh at his pilgrims he ensures that we remember who they are and what they look like.

CHANGES IN BOOK PRODUCTION

Paper and printing are introduced

When Chaucer died in 1400, book production was changing, and in the next 100 years the processes which you've just read about altered beyond belief. In 1400 paper was just beginning to be used instead of parchment. Twenty-five sheets of it (called a quire) cost the same as one animal skin but they provided eight times more writing space. By 1500, it had become cheaper still, and about half of the books being produced were written on it.

Most radically, in 1476 Caxton introduced the printing press into England, and the technology of book-making altered completely. In 1478 he produced his first edition of *The Canterbury Tales*. He reprinted it in 1485 and it has been in print ever since.

Bookmaking goes commercial

In London, in the fifteenth-century, the book-making industry took off and the works of the important poets of the day started to be reproduced commercially in multiple copies. Rather than making a copy of *The Canterbury Tales* when someone came in wanting one, it looks as though copies were being made in advance and customers could just come in and buy one for the first time.

As more and more people were able to read, customer demand eventually reached a level where commercial production was worthwhile. Even the Royal Court wanted to read texts in English, instead of ordering French books from the continent, so they, too, bought (rather more expensive copies) of contemporary poetry. And, of course, there was finally a core of very good poets who had produced enough work for this expanding audience to buy: Gower, Lydgate and, most importantly, Chaucer.

HOW DID CHAUCER WORK?

There isn't very much evidence about Chaucer's working practices, but we do know how his contemporaries operated. They often wrote in response to commissions from rich and influential people like the individuals Chaucer knew through his employment at the Royal Court. *The Book of the Duchess* was written after the death of Blanche, wife of John of Gaunt, and although it is not clear how Gaunt was involved in the production of the poem, he was clearly Chaucer's patron in some sense. Patronage was very important to the production of medieval poetry, and poets were constantly trying to impress potential patrons. Chaucer's *The Legend of Good Women* was given to Queen Anne, possibly in a very lavish presentation copy as a plea for her patronage of his work.

Chaucer's audience

There were two different kinds of audience for Chaucer's poetry. The first was likely to be an intimate one, made up of courtly and influential people known to him. They would *hear* a performance of the text which included appropriate gestures and different voices, almost like a play. The second was probably unknown to the author, and they would have read the poem from a book, perhaps to another audience of people they knew, but also, increasingly in the fifteenth century, silently in their heads to themselves.

The developments in printing made it possible for more people to own books, and it was only then that 'silent reading', which we take for granted, became popular. Until this point poetry was very unlikely to have been enjoyed on the page, and this changes the way the poet would have used verse to communicate with his audience. Chaucer's poetry is flexible enough to work well in both kinds of context – as a lively performance and as an experience inside the reader's head.

CHAUCER'S EARLY REPUTATION

Chaucer as a propaganda tool

Fifteenth-century poets such as Lydgate, Hoccleve and Henryson praised Chaucer's work within their own poems, and this was partly for political reasons. Because the Lancastrian reign began fairly dubiously with Henry IV's deposition of Richard II, the new king needed to strengthen his own authority. Part of his answer was to create a sense of 'Englishness' – of national pride and tradition – which would support the new dynasty of kings. By encouraging loyal poets to celebrate Chaucer's work, Henry helped English to flourish. This made a clear break with the French language, and gave a distinct identity to the new regime.

In the introduction to Caxton's edition of *The Canterbury Tales* he called Chaucer a 'noble and grete philosopher… the whiche for his ornate wrytyng in our tongue may wel haue the name of a laureate poete'. He sees Chaucer's importance as lying in his development of English which, 'he by hys labour enbelysshyd, ornated, and made faire'. This shows the way in which Chaucer was important 70 years after

> **KEYWORDS**
>
> **Laureate:** literally, 'one who wins laurels'. The term refers to a poet who is officially rewarded in financial terms, usually by the monarch, for writing for special occasions.

his death – as a 'laureate'. As a **laureate** he becomes a model for other poets, an epitome of the way poets worked in the past. In other words he becomes a *dead* poet from an age when things were different. So Chaucer's reputation as a laureate poet is partly a result of Lancastrian propaganda, which simultaneously glorifies him and gives the new dynasty a ready-made history of artistic achievement.

The epitome of medieval poetry

In the sixteenth century, Chaucer was seen primarily as a courtly poet. In Elizabeth's reign, the cult of chivalry was revived and there was a great nostalgia for a medieval past of knights and their ladies and the rules of courtly love. Chaucer, odd as it seems to us, was sufficiently antique by then to provide the inspiration for such revivals. Spenser's epic poem *The Faerie Queene* was inspired by his predecessor's use of English, and Book 4 was devised as a completion of Chaucer's Squire's Tale. There were also dramatic adaptations of the Clerk's, Physician's, Knight's, Man of Law's and Franklin's Tales on the Elizabethan stage.

Knowing how Chaucer has been read in the past and what it is about his poetry that has interested readers since the fourteenth century, helps us to understand our own interests in relation to theirs.

✳ ✳ ✳SUMMARY✳ ✳ ✳

● Each book was unique when Chaucer was writing, and very expensive.

● The poems we read today have been shaped by fifteenth-century scribes and modern editors.

● Reading in the medieval period was a serious moral business, but the material was often humorous.

● Fifteenth-century developments in book-making, such as paper and print, made Chaucer's work more widely available.

● Chaucer was seen, especially by the Lancastrians, as the 'Father of English poetry', the first laureate poet.

7 Modern critical approaches

CHAUCER'S CHANGING REPUTATION

As you have already read, Chaucer's poetry was greatly admired by his medieval readers. His status as the poet who made English credible as a literary language lasted until at least the end of the sixteenth century. From the seventeenth century onwards, however, critical opinion was considerably more mixed. As English altered to become the language with which we are familiar today, Chaucer's poetry began to sound at first old-fashioned and then just unintelligible.

However, towards the end of the nineteenth century, things began to change for the better. A different set of people began to comment on Chaucer's work. Instead of other writers reading his poetry and saying what they, as writers, thought of it, scholars began to read it and offer a *specialist* opinion. In 1868 the Chaucer Society was founded, and between 1894 and 1897 the first scholarly edition of Chaucer's work was produced. The poems were now available for a wider audience to read.

THE BIRTH OF LITERARY CRITICISM

So how were these scholars analysing Chaucer's work? They were developing a new kind of analysis of literature, one which was being applied to English literature in general at the end of the nineteenth century, not just to Chaucer. This was literary criticism, and it was intended to provide a series of criteria by which literature could be evaluated. Rather than recording their individual judgements, these scholars attempted to assess writing in terms of general standards which could explain the effects of the piece of work. In other words, rather than simply saying it was 'good' or 'bad', they were able to analyse their reaction to it as a result of the subject matter, the style and the techniques employed by the writer.

Since these beginnings, criticism has developed considerably. It has had to deal with some difficult problems along the way. For instance, on what basis can you judge a text? Should a poem by Chaucer be seen in relation to the 'world outside the text', to the effect it has on the reader, to the ideas and opinions of the author? Or should it just be seen as a self-sufficient work, which is independent of all of these aspects? To read more about early criticism of Chaucer see Burrow, *Geoffrey Chaucer: A Critical Anthology* (Penguin, 1969).

Literary criticism and Chaucer studies

These issues have been the preoccupations of criticism in general, but criticism of Chaucer's work has had its own particular problems. Any kind of critical theory has been very slow to be applied to Chaucer studies. One of the reasons for this is that scholars have tended to insist that the medieval period is fundamentally different from any other. In order to read the texts from the original manuscripts, specialist palaeographical skills are needed to decipher different kinds of writing. Scholars have reinforced the idea that it is hard to understand these texts without extensive training in the history of the period, an understanding of the kinds of literature being produced, and the methods involved in their production.

As the past is so different, these scholars have said that modern theories cannot be applied to it because they would be anachronistic. This is a very important debate, because it affects the way we see Chaucer's work and that of his contemporaries. To what extent is the past the same as the present and to what extent different? If Chaucer's poetry is so much a product of the past that we need to reconstruct that past in order to understand and appreciate it, then why doesn't the same apply to Dickens? In other words, when does 'the past' really begin, the period when can we no longer take it for granted that people thought and wrote like 'us'?

The rest of this chapter will encourage you to think about the similarities and differences between the fourteenth century and the twenty-first, and about the many different ways of reading Chaucer – even the many different Chaucers – which those resemblances and contrasts produce. There are no firm conclusions here and many of the critical approaches outlined contradict one another. Once you are aware of the basic issues involved in the debates you can go on and read the work of the critics who discuss them, and there are suggestions for further reading in each section. This chapter is organized around the same themes as the previous one, so that you can assess the ways in which modern criticism has dealt with those topics.

CHIVALRY AND HISTORICISM

When criticism of Chaucer's work began, scholars by and large tended to treat *The Canterbury Tales* as a document which they could read in order to see what life was like in the fourteenth century. This kind of criticism is often referred to as **traditional historicism**, and has since been criticized for its failure to see that literature does not represent life as it really is. The whole issue is more complicated than that. **New historicism** reacted against such a reading by stressing the fact that *all* texts, of whatever kind, are written with a particular purpose in mind and so offer *representations* of their historical moment rather than any unmediated access to reality. Unless we take into account the function a text is fulfilling for its contemporary writers and readers, new historicists remind us, we are likely to misread it entirely.

> **KEYWORDS**
>
> Traditional historicism: used literary texts as evidence of life in the past.
>
> New historicism: a critical movement which is interested in the ways texts are received by their readers.

This view of Chaucer's work is in many ways opposite to 'author-centred criticism'. In new historicism the author is seen as a product of his time, influenced by its ideologies and affected by other texts circulating in that period. Rather than looking for the meaning which Chaucer intended in his works, new historicism recognizes a multiplicity of possible meanings for the text which depend on the knowledge and interests of the particular reader. Chaucer as a unique creative genius is displaced by the idea of the author as a kind of channel for the preoccupations of his age, which he more or less passively reproduces in his work.

Problems with new historicism

Critics of this approach see it as ignoring the power of individual authors to have a say about the period in which they live – to examine it critically. As a way of approaching texts it is also directly contradictory to the approach of older criticism which claimed that literary texts had their own unique language, different from 'everyday' language, and that they could therefore be studied in isolation from any knowledge of the period in which they were written.

In addition to these criticisms and differences, new historicist critics themselves saw problems with their analysis. In the 1980s and 90s they became much more **reflexive** in their criticism. They began to realize the awful truth that we will *never* be able to read these poems exactly as they were read in the medieval

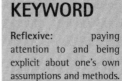

KEYWORD

Reflexive: paying attention to and being explicit about one's own assumptions and methods.

period. However much we know about that period, we will still never think, feel, listen or read like medieval men and women.

On the one hand this can be depressing because it means that all our efforts to see the original meaning of the texts are at best limited and at worst plain wrong. On the other hand, though, knowing this we can be honest about it – we can read in the knowledge that we are biased by our own times and their unique preoccupations. We can balance our interests in aspects of Chaucer's work which speak to our contemporary anxieties against issues with which we know his original audience were concerned. The next two sections of this chapter have more to say about this.

Different kinds of historicism

There are many different ways of relating Chaucer's work to the period in which he was writing because there are many different 'histories' of any given period. There are readings of his works which relate them to particular events in the fourteenth century and to particular kinds of medieval knowledge: intellectual or scientific for instance. If you are interested in reading examples of these approaches, try Wasserman and Blanch eds., *Chaucer in the Eighties* (Syracuse University Press, 1986). Then there are histories of mentalities, of the ways in which people *thought* in the period when Chaucer was writing. Here, too, there are differences – for instance, the way men and women think will be different.

If we are talking about the specific meanings of a particular part of one of Chaucer's poems, we have to try to appreciate (in the partial way suggested above) how it would have been understood by Chaucer's audience. This kind of enquiry links *all* the types of criticism discussed here through their common understanding of the importance of knowing how Chaucer's work would originally have been received.

The Knight's reputation

It is easier to see the issues involved using an example, and one such is the controversy over the portrait of the Knight in The General Prologue to *The Canterbury Tales*. The Knight had traditionally been seen as one of the few characters whom Chaucer described without a hint of irony, and of whom he was entirely approving. The portrait is characterized by the use of the word 'worthy', meaning both noble and well mannered, and is perhaps summed up in the statement that, 'He was a verray [true], parfit [complete] gentil kyght.

Two opposing views

In 1980 Terry Jones published a book called *Chaucer's Knight: Portrait of a Medieval Mercenary* (Weidenfeld and Nicolson), a deliberately provocative title. In it, he analysed the description which Chaucer gives and suggested that the way modern scholars had traditionally read it was very different from the way it would have been read by a medieval reader. He claims, based on an analysis of the battles at which the Knight is said to have fought, that the figure of the Knight is meant as an attack on the behaviour of the military men of Chaucer's own time.

In response, John H. Pratt wrote an article titled 'Was Chaucer's Knight Really a Mercenary?' in *The Chaucer Review* (Vol. 22, No. 1, 1987). In this article Pratt presents evidence which he feels proves the opposite point of view to Jones's, and, in doing so, he raises some vital points about the kind of questions we need to be asking of society in order to understand literature more fully.

What questions should we ask about the past?

At the beginning of Pratt's article he sets out to answer the following questions: What did Chaucer mean by certain geographical references? How much did Chaucer and his contemporary Englishmen know about foreign conflicts involving non-Christian combatants? What did Chaucer understand a crusade to be? Why does Chaucer employ certain military terminology? And, above all, is the omission of some geographical references as important as the inclusion of others?

These questions lead Pratt to employ several important kinds of **methodology**. Firstly, he needs to establish what Chaucer knew about crusades. So he discovers the legal definition of a just crusade and he reads the chronicle accounts of actual battles. It is then possible to

KEYWORD

Methodology: the interrelated group of methods used for a particular kind of analysis.

say what Chaucer and his readers *might* have known if they too were aware of these sources. From the legal evidence he is able to establish that Chaucer places his Knight at *legitimate* battles, those against the heathen Saracens.

One of the most important parts of Pratt's argument is his demonstration that the status of knighthood itself was a subject of concern when Chaucer was writing. This means that people reading about knights were likely to have in mind the kind of figure which Jones claims the Knight to be.

This all builds up to a very difficult question – when readers read about a character like the Knight, to what extent do they judge him by the things he *is* said to have done, and to what extent by those actions which he is *not* said to have performed? Readers often expect a familiar character to behave in a particular way. If the character behaves differently, this can have the effect of focusing the reader's mind on what they expected. If the character is completely different – the opposite of what they had anticipated – they may see the author's portrayal as ironic.

Locating Chaucer's writing in a period of change in the role of knighthood allows Pratt to conclude that the Knight, unlike his son the Squire, is likely to have been seen as a rather archaic figure – an ideal of knighthood from an earlier age which was thought at the time to be passing.

Pratt also discusses how the interests, concerns and knowledge of Chaucer's audience are likely to have shaped their attitudes towards the Knight. He points out that Chaucer's patrons, the men who promoted his poetry and lent the support of their status to his work, all identified themselves with those aims of chivalry which were discussed in the last chapter, and were strongly in favour of military adventure.

Pratt's defence of the Knight's reputation leads him and other critics like him to consider important questions about the relationship between literature and history – what issues were causing concern at the time? *Who* knew *what* about the subject and *how*? What is said and what is not said in the poem? In what ways is the poem influenced by its patrons and readers?

Finally, this is an interesting historicist debate partly because the whole idea of knighthood is very foreign to us. Most of us find it hard to imagine making a vow of solemn pious devotion to go to war against non-Christians. This is a mindset, a way of thinking, which we need the help of contemporary documents to imagine. However, we also need to hold on to that sense of incomprehension and to remember that concepts as seemingly universal as 'love', or 'work' could have an equally alien meaning in the medieval period.

If you are interested in reading more about the Knight, see Leicester, *The Disenchanted Self: Representing the Subject in the 'Canterbury Tales'* (University of California Press, 1990), and Patterson, *Chaucer and the Subject of History* (Routledge, 1991). For other historically aware readings of Chaucer see Brown and Butcher, *The Age of Saturn, literature and history in the Canterbury Tales* (Blackwell, 1991), and Brown, *Chaucer at Work: The Making of the Canterbury Tales* (Longman, 1994).

GENDER AND FEMINIST THEORY

There are clear links between feminist readings of Chaucer and new historicist concerns because both are arguing that we can understand Chaucer's work only if we try to comprehend medieval ways of thinking. **Feminist** critics are concerned with how women thought and felt in different periods of history. In order to uncover this, they try to

> **KEYWORDS**
>
> **Feminist:** a reading which focuses on the position of women within texts.
>
> **Patriarchy:** literally a social or political system governed by men.

identify the dominant ideologies which control meaning in texts – to draw attention to those ideas which are passed off as 'natural' or 'obvious' and to see whose interests it might be in to present them as such. For instance, they see an underlying negative attitude towards women in medieval texts which is often presented as a product of 'the way things are', or 'the way men and women are made'.

It is important to remember here the issues which were brought up about the authority of texts in this period in Chapter 6. Because what was written down was so strongly associated with 'truth', medieval ideologies were particularly pervasive. **Patriarchy** is a key concept for understanding the relations between the sexes in the medieval period, as it is an ideology which affected the way everybody then, and arguably now, thought about the differences between men and women. By trying to think outside patriarchal structures, feminism recovers and draws attention to the histories of women, who they see as both under- and mis-represented in medieval literature.

Feminist readings of Chaucer began by concentrating on the way women were portrayed as characters in the poems. This led to two important and divergent points of view about the author's own attitude towards women.

Was Chaucer a champion of women?

Some critics see Chaucer's work as taking a kind of proto-feminist stand – in other words they see the poems as presenting women in a much more favourable light than the works of many of his contemporaries. They see his writings as expressing an explicit, self-conscious interest in the contemporary debate about the relative nature of men and women – one which aims at social change.

These critics obviously focus on the Wife of Bath as a key piece of evidence in their argument. As we saw in the last chapter, the Wife embodies the debate about women – she is at the same time the epitome of women's supposed faults and an engaging and appealing character. Through the Wife's emphasis on 'experience', feminist critics argue that Chaucer was trying to present an alternative to male controlled authority. In doing so, they see not only the poems but Chaucer himself as actively challenging the accepted role and importance of women.

In this reading, the Wife of Bath is both a feminist critic of her society and a tool by which Chaucer hopes to change the situation of women for the better. Chaucer is seen here as trying to position himself as a woman – he is thought to be trying to imagine what it would be like to think and feel as a woman. On this subject, see Diamond and Edwards eds. (Massachusetts: 1988); Mann, *Geoffrey Chaucer* (Harvester Wheatsheaf, 1991); Cox, *Gender and Language in Chaucer* (Florida, 1997); Van, 'False texts and disappearing women in the Wife of Bath's prologue and Tale', *Chaucer Review*, 29, 1994; Evans and Johnson, *Feminist Readings in Middle English Literature* (Routledge, 1994); and Patterson, *Chaucer and the Subject of History* (Routledge, 1991).

Was Chaucer a patriarchal observer?

Other critics are more cynical. For example, it has been suggested earlier in this book that there are significant contrasts between the Knight's Tale and the Miller's. However, a feminist reading of *The Canterbury Tales* is likely to focus on similarity rather than difference, and critics have seen *both* tales as marginalizing women. In both tales the woman is merely an object in relation to which men work out their rivalries and try to better one another. Feminist critics see little interest on Chaucer's part in either woman's wishes, as neither tale examines which suitor she would have preferred.

This more cynical approach also sees problems with the portrayal of the Wife of Bath. Critics do agree that she is a parody of the anti-feminist view of women, and that by claiming the authority of experience she is challenging male control over social and intellectual life. It is then possible to view this as an attempt to portray an exciting world of possibility which could enable social change by empowering women with a set of alternatives to patriarchy. *Or* it is possible to see the Wife as a grotesque parody which is meant as a warning, as a fantastic collage of different kinds of anti-feminist text which has the aim of reminding the reader how important patriarchal structures are in stopping women acting in this kind of way. To read more about this view, try Dinshaw, *Chaucer's Sexual Politics*, (Madison, 1989); Crane, *Gender and Romance in Chaucer's Canterbury Tales*, (Princeton, 1994); Wilson, 'Chaucer and St Jerome: the use of "barley" in the Wife of Bath's Prologue', *Chaucer Review*, 19, 1985; Olson, *The Canterbury Tales and the Good Society*, (Princeton, 1986); and Hansen, *Chaucer and the Fictions of Gender* (Berkeley, 1992).

Developments in gender theory

Recently there have been further developments in the study of gender in Chaucer. From female characters, the debate has opened up to include gender *identity* – the gendered positions which men or women can adopt in relation to each other. This approach has been influenced by the work of Judith Butler in *Gender Trouble* (Routledge, 1990), or

Bodies that Matter (Routledge, 1993) on the concept of the 'performance' of gender as a series of learned actions and behaviours which define the differences between men and women. For readings of Chaucer influenced by this subject, see Hansen, *Chaucer and the Fictions of Gender* (Berkeley, 1992).

There have been other recent expansions of the field: in the growing area of masculinity studies, critics try to evaluate the influences of patriarchy on the way men behave. **Queer theory** has begun to pay attention to the portrayal of relationships between people of the same sex, and has produced important work on the construction of sexuality in this

> **KEYWORD**
>
> Queer theory: a critical approach which concentrates on same-sex relationships and on sexuality as specific to different societies and cultures.

period. This kind of analysis develops the work on gender by taking as its starting point the idea that our sexuality is not 'natural', not something we are born with, but rather a feature of the kind of society in which we live. For further information on these areas see Beidler ed., *Masculinites in Chaucer, Approaches to Maleness in the Canterbury Tales and Troilus and Criseyde* (D. S. Brewer, 1998), and Sturges, *Chaucer's Pardoner and Gender Theory* (Macmillan, 2000).

The issues raised by this type of criticism are important ones. They force us to ask ourselves whether we think Chaucer is a typical fourteenth-century man, reflecting the society in which he lives, or whether he is a radical writer, shaping the way society would advance. They also demand that we ask ourselves how we *know* whether a writer is being subversive or whether he is reinforcing the status quo.

For a general overview of this type of criticism, see Evans and Johnson, *Feminist Readings in Middle English Literature* (Routledge, 1994). If you are interested in knowing more about women in this period, see Blamires, *Woman Defamed, Woman Defended*, (Oxford, 1992) for concepts of the female in other medieval writings, and Goldberg, *Woman is a Worthy Wight* (Alan Sutton, 1992) for a historical account of the experiences of medieval women.

'OPEN' AND 'CLOSED' TEXTS AND THE IDEA OF COMMUNITY

Responses to Chaucer's representation of community offer another direction in criticism, invariably of *The Canterbury Tales*, which seeks to investigate issues of social power and social change. It is an approach which concentrates its analysis on the form of the poem itself, rather than the characters which are portrayed within it.

The new historicist approach tended to minimize the importance of Chaucer as an author, concentrating instead on his more or less subconscious presentation of issues of social concern in his works. This kind of investigation, however, suggests a very self-conscious author who intentionally offers a particular view of the society in which he writes. What that view might be forms the subject of considerable debate, however.

The Canterbury Tales and Mikhail Bakhtin

All critics agree that *The Canterbury Tales* is unfinished, and that the tales are made up of many different voices, styles of narration, speech and poetic form. This book has highlighted some of these differences in previous chapters. But the open-ended debate, the resistance to offering certain conclusions, and the contradictory truths which are offered within the tales have been viewed in two ways. Some critics have seen this as liberating and open-minded in its approach. Others, however, have felt that it is merely indecisiveness on Chaucer's part, and a reluctance to assert any one point of view.

Critics on both sides of this debate have been influenced by (amongst other things) the work of the literary theorist Mikhail Bakhtin on the relationship of different kinds of writing to the ideological conditions under which they are written. Bakhtin identified two kinds of text, the **monologic** and the **dialogic**. Monologic texts, he said, appear to be authoritative – they tell you the 'right way' of thinking about issues

KEYWORDS

Dialogic texts offer several different points of view without privileging any one in particular.

Monologic texts are didactic texts which give the reader a clear idea of the point of view they should adopt.

and close down debate on the subject. Dialogic texts, on the other hand, do not tell the reader what to think, instead they offer several ways of approaching issues, none of which appears to be privileged over any of the others. Bakhtin suggests several ways in which such texts undermine authority, and you can read more about them in his book *The Dialogic Imagination* (Austin, 1992). Their specific relevance to Chaucer is also usefully explained in Rigby, *Chaucer in Context* (Manchester, 1996).

Chaucer's 'conservative' poem

The series of portraits with which The General Prologue opens is, as has already been stressed, a representation of a social system. As such, it has implications for the way critics have thought about Chaucer's views on power, authority and hierarchy. Those who see *The Canterbury Tales* as a monologic text use the Prologue as evidence that Chaucer saw the current ordering of society as divinely ordained. They take the view that he was either representing a pre-existing order with which everyone was content, or that the situation was in fact very different, and the poem was an attempt to portray an ideal which papered over the social cracks on behalf of those in power.

Seeing Chaucer's writing in the context of the social, political, religious and economic changes and conflicts outlined in the 'Biography and social background' section, critics such as Burrow in his *Ricardian Poetry* (Penguin, 1992) have found The General Prologue invidiously conservative in its apparent search for the perfect social hierarchy. They agree that the work offers all the different kinds of linguistic and stylistic diversity outlined above, but they cannot agree that it offers the same variety of *ideological* approaches to social issues. Many of these critics also feel they can identify Chaucer's point of view within the work, and they see it as that put forward by socially conservative tales such as the Knight's. Other critics who see the poem as conservative, however, view the fact that no one opinion is paramount within the tales as evidence that Chaucer was unwilling to commit himself to changing society by taking a stand.

If you want to read more about the conservative *Canterbury Tales*, try Wood's essay in Yeager, *Chaucer and Gower: Difference, Mutuality and Exchange* (Victoria, 1991), Delany, *Medieval Literary Politics* (Manchester, 1990), or Olson, *The Canterbury Tales and the Good Society* (Princeton, 1996).

Chaucer's 'radical' poem

KEYWORD

Didacticism: having the intention to instruct, and the manner of a teacher.

On the other side, critics point to the lack of **didacticism** in the poem – to the fact that readers appear to be able to make up their own mind which pilgrim's world view to accept. They draw attention to the intentional confusion of authority in the text between Chaucer the author and Chaucer the pilgrim, one which unsettles the reader and makes them question who to believe. For these critics, the contradictory social opinions which *The Canterbury Tales* contain undermine the authority of any one point of view. Those who are usually marginalized in society, such as women for instance, are given an equal opportunity to tell a story. This view tends *not* to concentrate on The General Prologue, and it denies that any of the opinions presented in the poem can be identified with Chaucer's.

Seeing *The Canterbury Tales* in this way makes it possible to read them as antihierarchical, suggesting that Chaucer was examining social differences (such as those between knights and millers which were discussed above) in a way which wasn't possible in other types of writing because it would have been seen as subversive. It means imagining a Chaucer who could see beyond the hierarchies of his own world to a different kind of community where individuals were valued for their contribution to social harmony rather than for their birth and status. It is the 'radical Chaucer' again.

If you want to follow up this argument, see in the first instance Mann, *Chaucer and Medieval Estates Satire* (Cambridge, 1973), whose work in many ways made this debate possible; then see Aers, *Chaucer* (Brighton, 1986), Knapp, *Chaucer and the Social Contest* (New York,

1990), Strohm, *Social Chaucer* (Indiana, 1989), and Leicester in Ellis, *Chaucer, The Canterbury Tales* (Longman, 1998).

As these two views are so diametrically opposed, Rigby, in *Chaucer in Context*, attempts to find a way of resolving the opposition. He does so by trying to reconstruct the original audience reception of the poem in order to see what Chaucer thought he was doing. This allows us to see the differences in our reading of the text and the fourteenth-century one, based on an analysis of the different mentalities suggested by new historicism and investigated by feminism and gender studies.

PLACES TO START WITH CHAUCER CRITICISM

There are several very approachable summaries of current criticism on Chaucer's work available at the moment which offer a straightforward place to start. See, for instance, Rigby, *Chaucer in Context*; Brown, *Chaucer at Work*; Rudd, *The Complete Critical Guide to Geoffrey Chaucer* (Routledge, 2001); or Ellis, *Chaucer, The Canterbury Tales* (Longman, 1998), which has extracts from many of the important works cited above. All these books provide very detailed bibliographies which allow you to follow up the work of the critics they mention.

✳ ✳ ✳ *SUMMARY* ✳ ✳ ✳

● Contemporary critical debate about Chaucer is often contradictory.

● New historicism sees Chaucer as a product of the fourteenth century, and recognizes a multiplicity of meanings for his poems.

● This approach stresses the difference between medieval and modern mentalities.

● Feminist criticism of Chaucer is divided between views of him as a proto-feminist and a patriarchal observer.

● Critics of Chaucer have been influenced by Bakhtin's distinctions between monologic and dialogic texts.

● Criticism of the attitude towards community in *The Canterbury Tales* is divided between seeing a radical Chaucer pushing for change and a conservative poet trying to maintain existing social structures.

Where to next?

TAKE A ROUTE AROUND CHAUCER'S POEMS

The Canterbury Tales is a good place to begin reading because its structure divides it neatly into sections. You can use it as a route into Chaucer's many other long and short poems. Think about the aspects of his work which have interested you so far – the kinds of subject matter which you have enjoyed reading about (depictions of women or knights or gardens perhaps); or the genre which has appealed to you (romances or fabliaux for instance).

Then invest in an edition of Chaucer's complete works which has a really good glossary and footnotes to help you to translate difficult words. The best is probably *The Riverside Chaucer* (Larry D. Benson, ed., OUP, 1988). This is an absolute bargain, with notes which are easy to follow and further commentary at the back if you want to know more.

It can be very illuminating and pleasurable to listen to Chaucer on audio tape or CD. A good reader can bring the text to life and add a flavour of the times. Pavillion Records Audiobooks seem to cover most of the tales and their prologues.

Here are some suggestions, some obvious, some more unusual, for routes which you might take around a Chaucer anthology:

An obvious choice is to read poems about love and longing. You could begin with the short poem 'Chaucer's Complaint to his Lady', go on to read the Knight's Tale, and then *Troilus and Criseyde*. These are all courtly love poems, so as a contrast you could look at the Merchant's Tale, which is a very bawdy fabliau. This will show you a different representation of medieval love!

If it is winter rather than spring, or you're not in the mood for love, try reading poems about another medieval preoccupation – death. 'The Complaint to Pity' connects love to death, and you could go from there to *The Book of the Duchess*, a dream vision about a bereaved lover. The Pardoner's Tale is also interesting here – a ghastly allegory of man's relationship with death.

If that sounds rather heavy, how about medieval animals as a topic? Read The General Prologue to *The Canterbury Tales* and see how much you can learn about the pilgrims from the description of their horses, and the other information about their attitudes to animals which Chaucer tells the reader. You could read the description of Alison in the Miller's Tale, and think about the use made of animal comparisons, and then go on to the Nun's Priest's Tale and the Manciple's Tale, which are types of beast fable. Finally, there is the *Parliament of Fowls*, which takes you back to the theme of love again.

Or how about gardens: study their representation in the Knight's, the Merchant's and the Franklin's Tales, and in *The Romaunt of the Rose*. Then read Howes, *Chaucer's Gardens and the Language of Convention* (Florida University Press, 1997) for some ideas about their interpretation.

One last suggestion is medieval science. The astrological setting of The General Prologue is a good place to start, and if you want more information about astronomy and astrology in this period, Book VII of John Gower's *Confessio Amantis* is a useful guide. Then there is the Canon Yeoman's Tale of strange alchemical practices, and finally *A Treatise on the Astrolabe* – Chaucer says that he's writing it at the request of his ten-year-old son Lewis, to teach him how the astrolabe measures the altitude of the stars.

READ THE CRITICS
Reading critical works about Chaucer's poems will help to deepen your own understanding of the way they work. In addition to the works mentioned in the previous chapter, there are several good

introductions, for instance Mann, *The Cambridge Chaucer Companion* (Cambridge University Press, 1986) or Blamires, *The Canterbury Tales* (Macmillan, 1987) which discuss modern criticism of the poem. If you want to know more about Chaucer himself, Derek Pearsall's biography, *The Life of Geoffrey Chaucer* (Blackwell, 1992) describes every scrap of evidence for his life in loving detail.

LEARN MORE ABOUT THE PERIOD
If you would like to know more about the England in which Chaucer lived, there are lots of exciting ways to do this. There are books about the medieval period, such as Rigby, *English Society in the Later Middle Ages* (Basingstoke, 1995), or M. H. Keen's *England in the Later Middle Ages* (Methuen, 1973).

Or you could watch a video: Simon Schama's recent dramatic *History of Britain* series takes you through the main political events of the period using contemporary medieval images in conjunction with footage of the important locations and buildings involved.

EXPLORE THE INTERNET
The internet boasts an enormous amount of sites about Chaucer and the world in which he lived. There are several excellent sources of other texts written in the medieval period. For instance the Middle English Text Archive:

http://etext.lib.virginia.edu/mideng.browse.html

or the Medieval Sourcebook:

http://www.fordham.edu/halsall/sbook.html

If you're interested in medieval images, you could try this website of woodcuts from contemporary books:

http://www.godecookery.com/clipart/fish/clfish.htm medieval woodcuts

Or for a truly multimedia medieval experience, you could visit the Luminarium site:

http://www.luminarium.org/

Harvard University gives Chaucer his very own homepage, and this has excellent background information, and a whole section of sound clips of people speaking Chaucer's poetry with the proper medieval intonation:

http://icg.fas.harvard.edu/~chaucer/index.html

For wider historical contexts, see the Discovery Channel website. You can follow a rat through a series of pages which bring the Black Death to life!

http://www.discovery.com/stories/history/blackdeath/instructions.html

HAVE A 'CHAUCER ADVENTURE'!

Go one stage further and take a historical walk around London or Canterbury. You could visit the South Bank of the Thames, starting at the end of London Bridge where the pilgrims began their journey to Canterbury. The medieval bridge is long gone but the road is still in the same place as it was then, and you can imagine Henry V coming back from Agincourt down it, or Wat Tyler's rebellion mustering there for their attack on the city. A few minutes' walk down the road is the site of the Tabard Inn from which the pilgrims left, in Borough High Street.

If you walk west along the riverbank you will come to the medieval Southwark cathedral. A modern window depicts the pilgrims setting out for Canterbury, next to the splendid medieval tomb of Chaucer's friend the poet John Gower. His effigy lies under a canopy, the head resting on his *Confessio Amantis*, the book commissioned by King Richard.

Further on is the Bishop of Winchester's London palace, from which Thomas Becket left on his final journey to Canterbury; and the Clink Museum which records the gory history of a notorious prison whose dungeons were below the high tide level of the Thames.

Going back to the road, you can travel to the medieval city of Canterbury, following the route which the pilgrims took. Once you reach the town, the tourist information centre has leaflets about several walks which take you around the city walls with their towers and bastions, and the gates which were paid for by Archbishop Sudbury, murdered in the Peasants' Revolt. You can see old monasteries, pilgrim inns, hospitals for the sick, and even ancient privies.

In the cathedral you can follow in the steps of the sacred journey Chaucer's company took, past the site of the martyrdom of Becket, to the place where the elaborate and glittering shrine used to stand. This part of the cathedral has huge medieval stained glass windows which show narratives of the miracles which took place after Becket's death.

Finally, to see Chaucer's poem come to life, visit The Canterbury Tales Experience. Every sense is catered for in this modern re-creation of some of the most famous tales, with models of the characters, a soundtrack of the story, and authentic medieval smells!

If you can't visit in person, you can take a virtual tour over the internet, to Southwark:

http://www.hhhconsulting.co.uk/southbank/

Its cathedral:

http://dswark.org/cathedral/tour/explore.htm

Or Canterbury:

http://www.hillside.co.uk/tour/tour.html

READ CHAUCER'S CONTEMPORARIES
As so few works survive from this period, it is often rewarding to try to understand Chaucer's poetry in relation to that of his contemporary writers, some of whom you have heard of from other chapters in this book. You can go on to pursue the issues which have interested you in Chaucer in their work. For instance, you could read Boccacio's

Decameron if you have enjoyed the structure of *The Canterbury Tales,* as this work is also a collection of stories told by a party of people, in this case elite men and women who have left the town to escape the plague in the countryside.

Or you could try John Gower's *Confessio Amantis,* also a collection of stories, this time connected by the theme of love. One of them is a version of the same tale which the Wife of Bath tells, and the text as a whole, contains a passage in praise of his friend Chaucer.

If you enjoyed the example of alliterative verse in the section entitled 'How did Chaucer develop the English language?' in Chapter 3, then try reading more of *Gawain and the Green Knight.* As well as being a tale of warfare, strange green pagan figures and seductive ladies, it is also a beautifully crafted poem with a very clever structure and a surprise ending.

✳ ✳ ✳*SUMMARY*✳ ✳ ✳

- Find a route around Chaucer's poems which interests you.

- Read the critics.

- Learn more about the period with books, videos or the internet.

- Have a 'Chaucer adventure'.

- Read Chaucer's contemporaries.

GLOSSARY

Allegory   A narrative which can be understood on several different levels.

Alliterative verse   Poetry in which consonants or stressed syllables are repeated.

Dialogic   texts offer several different points of view without privileging any one in particular.

Didacticism   Having the intention to instruct, and the manner of a teacher.

Dream vision   A device in medieval writing where the narrator goes to sleep and 'dreams' the work.

Estates satire   The use of stereotype to show the worst or best of different occupations or ranks.

Fabliau   A short comic or satiric tale, often of middle-class life, often fairly obscene.

Feminist   A reading which focuses on the position of women within texts.

Gawain and the Green Knight   A fourteenth-century alliterative poem about a large green knight who challenges Gawain to a beheading game on New Year's Day.

Genre   A kind, form, or type of literature with its own unique set of stylistic features.

Historicist   A reading which assumes that literary products are determined by the period in which they were written.

Irony   Expression of meaning in language which seems to suggest the opposite.

Intertextuality   A relationship between texts where the language, themes, images or ideas of one text are alluded to in another.

Laureate   Literally, 'one who wins laurels'. The term refers to a poet who is officially rewarded in financial terms, usually by the monarch, for writing for special occasions.

Lollardy   Fourteenth-century heretical beliefs in a variety of corruptions in the organization and worship of the medieval Catholic Church.

Methodology   The interrelated group of methods used for a particular kind of analysis.

Monologic   texts are didactic texts which give the reader a clear idea of the point of view they should adopt.

New historicism   A critical movement which is interested in the ways texts are received by their readers.

Traditional historicism   used literary texts as evidence of life in the past.

Patriarchy   Literally a social or political system governed by men.

Pilgrimage   A religiously motivated journey to the shrine of a saint.

Poll tax   A 'head' tax, levied on every person within a community, regardless of their wealth.

Queer theory   A critical approach which concentrates on same-sex relationships and on sexuality as specific to different societies and cultures.

Realism   A difficult and elastic term, usually taken to mean the presentation of life as it is. In this sense it is the opposite of an ideal representation. It can also mean the *appearance* of reality in a text.

Reflexive   Paying attention to and being explicit about one's own assumptions and methods.

Romance   A narrative of courtly and chivalrous behaviour, usually involving a quest and often containing supernatural elements.

Subversive   Seeking or tending to overthrow or upset the prevailing social order.

Type   A person or character who serves as a representative of a group of people.

Chronology of major works

Dates relating to Chaucer's life are in bold.

1340s	**Early in the decade Chaucer was born in London.**
1348–9	The Black Death reaches the shores of England.
1357	**Chaucer is a page in the household of the Countess of Ulster, wife of Lionel, the son of Edward III.**
1359–60	**Joins the retinue of Prince Lionel of France, and is captured and ransomed at the siege of Reims.**
1365/6	**Marries Philippa, daughter of a member of Queen Philippa's household and sister to John of Gaunt's future wife.**
1366	**Chaucer's father dies and his mother remarries. Goes on a diplomatic mission to Navarre (Spain). Son Thomas probably born.**
Late 1360s	Translates the *Roman de la Rose*.
1368	**Goes abroad on the King's service.** Writes *The Book of the Duchess* after the death of Blanche, John of Gaunt's first wife.
1369–70	**Goes to France with an expeditionary force.**
1372	**Philippa Chaucer granted an annuity by John of Gaunt for service in the household of the Duchess Constance, his second wife.**
1376	**Death of the Black Prince, Chaucer negotiates for peace and the King's marriage.**
1377	Death of Edward III, accession of Richard II.
1378	**Chaucer in Italy on diplomatic business.**
1380	**Son Lewis born.** C.1380-1 writes *The Knight's Tale* and *The Parliament of Fowls*.
1381	**Chaucer's mother dies.** Writes *Troilus and Criseyde* and The Peasants' Revolt.
1385	**Receives livery of mourning as esquire of the King's household on the death of Joan of Kent, the King's mother.**
1386	**Made MP for Kent. Resigns from the customs.**
1387	**Death of Philippa Chaucer.** C.1386-7 *The Legend of Good Women* written; Begins *The Canterbury Tales*; John Gower begins his *Confessio Amantis*.
1389	**Appointed Clerk of the King's Works.**
1390	**Robbed of the King's money on the highway.**
1391	*A Treatise on the Astrolabe* **is written. Resigns as Clerk of the Works.**
1394	**Receives a royal annuity of £20.**
1395/6	**Receives a fine scarlet gown from the future Henry IV.**
1397	**Receives royal grant of a tun of wine a year.**
1399	Death of John of Gaunt. Deposition of Richard II, accession of Henry IV.
1400	**Writes** *The Complaint of Chaucer to his Purse*. **Dies and is buried in Westminster Abbey and moved in 1556 to become the first tenant of 'Poet's Corner'.**

INDEX